# Metaphor, Riddles, and the Origin of Language

# Metaphor, Riddles, and the Origin of Language

## The Sphinx's Legacy

Marcel Danesi

LEXINGTON BOOKS
*Lanham • Boulder • New York • London*

Published by Lexington Books
An imprint of The Rowman & Littlefield Publishing Group, Inc.
4501 Forbes Boulevard, Suite 200, Lanham, Maryland 20706
www.rowman.com

86-90 Paul Street, London EC2A 4NE

Copyright © 2023 by The Rowman & Littlefield Publishing Group, Inc.

*All rights reserved.* No part of this book may be reproduced in any form or by any electronic or mechanical means, including information storage and retrieval systems, without written permission from the publisher, except by a reviewer who may quote passages in a review.

British Library Cataloguing in Publication Information Available

**Library of Congress Cataloging-in-Publication Data**

Names: Danesi, Marcel, 1946- author.
Title: Metaphor, riddles, and the origin of language : the sphinx's legacy / Marcel Danesi.
Description: Lanham : Lexington Books, [2022] | Includes bibliographical references and index. | Summary: "This book contributes to the debate surrounding the origin of language by demonstrating that riddles and myths can be examined as evidence of the emergence of conceptual metaphors, a prerequisite for the development of a complete language"— Provided by publisher.
Identifiers: LCCN 2022036928 (print) | LCCN 2022036929 (ebook) | ISBN 9781666918199 (cloth) | ISBN 9781666918205 (epub) | ISBN 9781666918212 (paperback)
Subjects: LCSH: Language and languages—Origin. | Metaphor. | Riddles.
Classification: LCC P116 .D35 2022  (print) | LCC P116  (ebook) | DDC 401—dc23/eng/20220808
LC record available at https://lccn.loc.gov/2022036928
LC ebook record available at https://lccn.loc.gov/2022036929

# Contents

| | |
|---|---|
| List of Figures | vii |
| List of Tables | ix |
| Introduction | 1 |
| Chapter One: Riddles and Language | 5 |
| Chapter Two: Riddle Functions | 35 |
| Chapter Three: Poetic Logic | 61 |
| Chapter Four: Riddles and Conceptual Metaphors | 83 |
| Chapter Five: Language Origins | 109 |
| References | 129 |
| Index | 143 |
| About the Author | 147 |

# List of Figures

| | |
|---|---|
| Figure 1.1 A Mythic Riddle Dichotomy | 17 |
| Figure 1.2 Interactionist Model of Metaphor | 24 |
| Figure 1.3 Metaphorical Clustering | 28 |
| Figure 3.1 Genesis of Metaphor Based on Vico | 62 |
| Figure 3.2 Vico's *Corso* of History | 65 |
| Figure 3.3 A Poetic Logic Model of the Riddle of the Sphinx | 72 |
| Figure 4.1 Riddle Mappings | 86 |
| Figure 4.2 Blending | 89 |
| Figure 4.3 Layering | 97 |
| Figure 5.1 A Model of Riddle Solving | 119 |
| Figure 5.2 The Metaphor Hypothesis | 125 |

# List of Tables

| | |
|---|---|
| Table 1.1 Riddle Functions | 13 |
| Table 1.2 Riddles and Conceptual Metaphor Theory | 27 |
| Table 1.3 Reconstructed Words | 32 |
| Table 2.1 Phenomenological Riddles | 41 |
| Table 5.1 Speech and Language | 110 |
| Table 5.2 Parallel Views of Levels | 121 |

# Introduction

One of the most intriguing questions that has fascinated humans since the dawn of history is how language originated. With the rise of philology as a precursor to contemporary linguistics in the early nineteenth century, the study of this question became an all-consuming one, so much so that in 1866 the Linguistic Society of Paris imposed a ban on all discussions related to this topic. A similar prohibition was put into place by the Philological Society of London a little later in 1872. Such drastic actions were motivated by the endless speculations, conjectures, and unfounded origin scenarios that were bandied about at the time. For almost a century thereafter, language scientists tended to shy away from engaging in any kind of debate or research related to the seemingly insoluble enigma of the phylogenesis of language and speech. This situation changed by the early 1970s, as a result of the suggestive research that was being conducted in such interrelated fields as archeology, paleography, ethology, psychology, neurology, anthropology, semiotics, and linguistics—all of which shed empirical light on specific areas of a language origins scenario.

Today, much is known about how speech—as a neural and physiological capacity—emerged as an evolutionary consequence of bipedalism and brain expansion in early hominid species. This line of research has largely resolved *how* the vocal apparatus evolved to permit speech as the capacity to name things, that is, to assign vocal labels to them for referential purposes. However, little remains known about how this naming capacity developed into full-blown language, defined as the ability to conceptualize not only about the things named, but about their connections to the other aspects of reality, and thus to contemplate questions about their nature and *raison d'être*. Albeit highly reductive and certainly artificial, this distinction between *speech* and *language* will be utilized in this book. It is used here for the sake of argument as a difference between the capacity to name things versus the capacity to understand them. Hypothetically, this distinction might provide a basis upon which to examine the origin of language as a conceptual system, rather than just a referential (name-based) system.

Scientific evidence for the origin of speech is abundant; but evidence for the origin of language as separate from speech as a naming system remains as speculative as it was during the nineteenth century. The main problem that plagued the early philologists remains to this day: What evidence can be utilized or accessed that will furnish relevant insights to draft a scenario for the origin of language as a means to *think* about the world, not just *name* it? This book attempts to provide a tentative answer to this question by suggesting that the first riddles of humanity, along with the first myths, reveal how language might have emerged as a mode of reflection via metaphor—a mode that involves blending speech forms together to produce complex, abstract cognition. The premise put forward in this book is, therefore, that metaphor first made its appearance in riddles and the myths that enfolded them.

The Riddle of the Sphinx constitutes one of the earliest—if not *the* earliest—riddle that has been documented in human history. As will be discussed throughout this book, it constitutes the kind of philological evidence required for validating the above *metaphor hypothesis*, since it highlights how metaphor emerged as an imaginative strategy for understanding abstractions in terms of something that has been experienced concretely. The Sphinx's Riddle is thus both the departure point and the end point for this book. Its structure and intent provide a blueprint for separating language from the naming functions of speech. The latter are not unlike the signal systems of different species, which allow for reference to the immediate environment. On the other hand, there is little or no evidence that language, as a conceptual system, exists in any species other than the human one. The *metaphor hypothesis*, more precisely, is the claim that riddles, along with contemporaneous myths, were among the first expressive artifacts revealing how abstract concepts were forged via metaphor, thus putatively providing the missing link between speech and language.

Riddles coincide chronologically and thematically with the first myths—either embedded in them, as the Riddle of the Sphinx was in the Oedipus legend, or else constituting a kind of cognitive partnership with them, encoding the same set of concepts, such as *life* or *destiny*, on the basis of metaphor. While the social and cultural functions of the early riddles have been studied extensively, surprisingly there is no work analyzing what their emergence in human history implies for the origin of language. Cognitive linguists who see metaphor as the conceptual core of language (for example, Lakoff and Johnson 1980, 1999) have surprisingly never dealt with the metaphor hypothesis (as defined here), which can actually be used as a litmus test to substantiate their claim from an evolutionary perspective. Eve Sweetser's book, *From Etymology to Pragmatics* (1990), did break some important ground in this direction, applying conceptual metaphor theory to early language concepts. But, as far as can be told, there has been little or no follow-up work in this area—and certainly no work that deals specifically with riddles as the earliest examples of how metaphor undergirds the linguistic construction of abstract thinking. A primary goal of this book is to fill this gap, so as to determine if the early riddles do indeed provide sufficient evidence to support the view of cognitive linguists that metaphor is the conceptual backbone of language.

A secondary goal of this book is to chart the evolution of the social functions of riddles, which appears to be largely in step with the evolution of the discourse functions of language more generally. Riddles emerge as part of oral traditions, spoken by wise elders or oracles in early cultural settings, challenging people to think creatively about metaphysical notions; over time they started assuming ludic, pedagogical, and literary-aesthetic functions. So, while the early riddles were intended as cautionary, divinatory, or wise tales, constituting a mythic language all their own, the subsequent ones were designed primarily for delectation and pedagogy, devised with clever and ingenious metaphors. It is to be noted from the outset that it is impossible to discuss metaphor without resorting to metaphor—a fact that implicitly supports the metaphor hypothesis. As James Geary (2011) has so insightfully put it, "Metaphors hide in plain sight, and their influence is largely unconscious. We should mind our metaphors, though, because metaphors make up our minds."

The inspiration for this book comes from teaching two courses at the University of Toronto over several decades—one on the history of puzzles and another in linguistic anthropology. The topic of riddles and their connection to language origins came up constantly in those courses. This book is a result of the many discussions and interactions I had with students and, by extension, with colleagues in linguistics, anthropology, and semiotics. Needless to say, any infelicities that this book may contain are my sole responsibility. Hopefully, if nothing else, the importance of studying riddles as sources for examining the relation between language and thought will come through.

## Chapter One

# Riddles and Language

### PROLOGUE

Research on childhood verbal development has established that children around the age of five or six respond to riddles in relatively uniform ways across the world, regardless of language or culture (Yalisove 1978; Purser, Herwegen, and Thomas 2020). The relevant inference that can be drawn from such work for the present purposes is that riddle comprehension is not a learned culture-specific behavior but rather emerges spontaneously the instant children learn to use language in ways that transcend the simple referential naming function of words in isolation. In effect, children do not need to be taught what a riddle is—they know instinctively that it impels them to seek a nonobvious answer to the question it asks. The developmental research thus suggests strongly that riddles are universal features of the language-mind nexus—a fact that is further confirmed by the archeological-philological fact that the same kinds of riddles are found across ancient societies as part of their earliest folkloric and mythic traditions, prefiguring prose speech (Jaynes 1976). It would seem that language ontogeny does indeed recapitulate phylogeny.

In tandem, the developmental and philological-archeological research literatures provide a theoretically plausible rationale for examining riddles in terms of what they imply for the shift from the purely referential (naming) functions of speech to the abstract, conceptual functions of language. Moreover, since they are implanted on a primary form of metaphor (as will be discussed throughout this book), they also bear concrete implications for assessing the validity of current cognitive theories of language, especially those that envision metaphor as a core neural faculty guiding the formation of complex thoughts. As Edie (1976) pointed out a while back, the main assumption of such theories, which gained momentum in the mid-1970s, is that metaphor is a faculty of mind, not just of language, which manifests itself not only in everyday speech but in virtually all other areas of expression and cognition. In a nutshell, as the research in developmental psychology and in philology suggests, the ancient riddles can be used to test the *metaphor hypothesis*, as indicated in the introduction to this book, which implies that speech as a naming capacity, based on reference to the immediate environment, evolved into language when the speech forms were blended together imaginatively in the early riddles and myths, producing the first abstract concepts as the basis of complex thinking.

Even from a surface consideration of the early riddles, it becomes evident that they were devised as metaphors for metaphysical abstractions, long before these entered the realm of philosophical discourse. The Riddle of the Sphinx is perhaps the earliest case in point. According to legend, it was the mythic hero Oedipus who first solved the Sphinx's Riddle—but doing so at his own unwitting risk, since it ultimately led to the fulfilment of his tragic fate as proclaimed by the oracle at Delphi to his father at birth (discussed subsequently). The riddle is a metaphor for *life*, portrayed as a three-phase cycle (infancy-adulthood-old age) that is mapped conceptually against the three phases of the day (dawn-noon-twilight). As such, it provides an early (if not the earliest) view that human life and the passage of time are intrinsically interconnected, albeit in mysterious ways. The way in which it does so—via the metaphorical mapping—is the rationale for examining riddles in general as providing insights into the evolution of metaphor as the basis of language. It should be mentioned from the outset that the exact riddle asked by the Sphinx was not specified by the early tellers of the Oedipus myth, and it was not standardized until late in Greek history (Edmunds 1981). So, the one to be discussed here is taken from literary traditions.

Myths and legends such as the Oedipus one abound in antiquity, preceding what we now call narrative history and ontological philosophy. As such, they are manifestations of an inherent tendency to use a narrative frame (or perhaps "grammar") for making connections among referents that are felt or experienced to be meaningful and reflective of some underlying pattern, as Ernst Cassirer (1953) demonstrated persuasively, showing how myth reflected the emergence of an unconscious grammar, based on narrative connectivity, which evolved much later into the rational grammar of subsequent prose language. As Mâche (1993, 21) has also argued "myth seems more like a psychic content from which words radiate," with the psychic content being essentially equivalent to Cassirer's unconscious grammar.

As the ancient societies started moving away from their mythological mindset, riddling evolved in tandem, assuming new functions. One of these was recreation, as can be seen in the use of riddle competitions at feasts such as the Greek Symposium (Sebo 2009). By the fourth century CE, riddles had become widely utilized for their ludic value, having moved away from their previous function as prophetic mythic structures. In the same time frame, they also started assuming two additional functions—pedagogical and literary—as witnessed by the use of riddles to train early medieval students and by the publication of riddle collections in the same era that were crafted in a high literary-poetic style (Taylor 1951).

This chapter provides a schematic overview of the unique phenomenon of riddling, so as to lay the groundwork for exploring its implications for the metaphorical origins of conceptual language, thus allowing for an assessment of the view of cognitive linguists that metaphor is the conceptual backbone of language (Lakoff and Johnson 1980; Lakoff and Turner 1989; Fauconnier and Turner 2002; among others). The premise on which the metaphor hypothesis is founded is that riddles provide the earliest philological evidence of how the use of words as simple referential tools evolved into a system for understanding the very referents that the words encoded. It is somewhat surprising to find that research in cognitive linguistics has never focused on riddling as a basis of support of its main tenet, at least to the best of my knowledge. The overall objective in this book is to fill this gap in a suggestive way.

## BACKGROUND

Riddles emerge as part of ancient oral traditions across the world, likely devised and recited by wise elders and oracles. Many of these gradually became part of folklore, since they were eventually recorded with the advent and spread of writing. From the storehouse of riddle collections that has come down to us from antiquity, it is evident that their primary function was to make the emerging metaphysical concepts comprehensible in concrete ways, mirroring the same kind of narratively based knowledge function of their contemporaneous myths. For this reason, the early riddles can be called *mythic*, given that the metaphysical notions that they enfold are the same ones found in parallel myths.

The Riddle of the Sphinx is one of the earliest riddles that has come down to us in written form, going back to around 2500 BCE by most estimates. It encapsulates the central theme in the story of Oedipus the King—namely that *life*, like the *phases* of the day, unfolds in a fixed way that cannot be altered by human intervention. The riddle is found in various Greek dramas, including *Oedipus and the Sphinx* by Epicharmus of Kos (c. 460 BCE), and *Oedipus Rex* by Sophocles (c. 429 BCE). It is not stated explicitly in the latter play, but enlisted by allusion, suggesting that the audience knew it quite well. The relevant narrative context of all versions of the Sphinx's Riddle is as follows. When Oedipus approached the city of Thebes he encountered a gigantic sphinx guarding entrance to the city. The sphinx confronted him posing the following riddle to him, warning Oedipus that if he failed to answer it correctly, he would die instantly at its hands:

> What creature walks on all fours at dawn, two at midday, and three at twilight?

According to the legend, Oedipus's answer astonished the sphinx, which can be paraphrased as follows: "Humans, who crawl on all fours as babies, then walk on two legs as grown-ups, and finally need a cane in old age to get around." Upon hearing the correct answer, the sphinx killed itself and Oedipus was able to enter Thebes, hailed as a hero for having defeated the terrible monster that had kept the city in captivity for so long. There also exists a second Sphinx's Riddle, attributed to the poet Theodectes (c. 370 BCE) (Taplin 1985, 134; Kaplan 2020):

> There are two sisters: one gives birth to the other and she then gives birth to the first. (*Answer:* day and night)

The relevant aspect of both riddles is that they revolve around the notion of time as a continuous sequence of events. In the first, and best-known riddle, this conceptualization is based on a metaphorical connection between the *phases of life* (infancy-maturity-old age) to the *phases of a day* (morning-noon-night), and in the second on the metaphorical image of one event (day or night) giving *birth* to the other (night or day), as in a cycle.

It is to be noted that the exact same metaphors for time are found in riddles across the ancient world (Taylor 1948; Salomon 1996; Kaivola-Bregenhøj 2016; Seyeb-Gohrab 2010); strongly suggesting a conceptual strategy for grasping the intangible meaning of life as inextricably connected to the passage of time by mapping it against the concrete experience of the different phases of the day. Given their antiquity, since they precede Greek drama, by several millennia, the riddles provide intriguing evidence that they constituted an early form of "languaging," as Alton Becker (2000) calls it—that is, the ability to transform imaginative thoughts into language forms. The latter have been called *root metaphors* (Lent 2017), given that they find resonance across languages, even those that bear no phylogenetic relation to each other. They are also called *primary metaphors* (Grady 1997), defined by Lakoff and Johnson (1999, 23) as "fundamental metaphors that are shared across many cultures."

In sum, primary metaphors, such as the *phases of the day* one in the Riddle of the Sphinx are found across ancient cultures, portraying metaphysical notions in virtually the same ways (as will be discussed throughout this book). As the cultures started creating riddles for other purposes, such as for recreation, the metaphors became more and more situation based, becoming less and less understandable across cultures. This suggests that there are two main categories of metaphor (even if this is a reductive assessment for the present purposes): (1) primary metaphors, which are universally understandable even through translation; and (2) situation-specific metaphors, which are understood mainly in culturally based ways. The former are intrinsic to early riddles and myths, while the latter develop over time to serve specific types of discourse and social functions. In other words, as the ancient cultures evolved, so too did their reliance of primary metaphors. By the early medieval period, riddles based on situation-specific metaphors crop up everywhere, subserving new ludic, pedagogical, and literary functions.

One of the most famous collections of this type, is the *Aenigmata Symphosii*, from the fourth or fifth century CE—a compilation of one hundred riddles in the form of brief Latin epigrams (Sebo 2018). It was written by a certain Symphosius, about whom virtually nothing is known (to be discussed further in the next chapter). The following is a riddle from the *Aenigmata* (Symphosius, *The Hundred Riddles of Symphosius*, Internet Archive, https://archive.org/stream/hundredriddless00sympgoog/hundredriddless00sympgoog_djvu.txt):

> *A fox*
> My bravery exceeds my body's size,
> An adept in deceit and skilled in lies,
> A wise beast I, if any beast is wise.

The fact that the answer is given at the start suggests that riddles at the time were intended for someone to read out loud who, knowing the answer in advance, would presumably be better able to dramatize the riddle to listeners. As can be seen, the riddle hardly has the same type of metaphysical function or language based on a primary metaphorical conceptualization as in the Riddle of the Sphinx. Rather, it describes characteristics of a creature, challenging us to interpret them connectively in order to come up with the answer. It is an example of personification, whereby the fox is assigned the human role of narrator of the riddle, talking about itself in terms of human characteristics that are mapped onto the animal metaphorically—*bravery, deceit, skilled in lies, wisdom*. This metaphorical portrait of foxes as clever and deceitful is situation specific, found mainly in Western and Persian folkloric traditions—probably based on the fox's reputed ability to evade hunters. In Asian folklore, on the other hand, foxes are depicted as sacred creatures that can bring wonder or ruin (Uther 2006). In Chinese legends, foxes are seen as bearers of a good or a bad omen, depending on context and particular occasion (Kang 2006). In such societies, Symphosius's riddle would resist the required answer, and seem somewhat unusual.

In the preface to the collection, it is stated that the riddles were designed to be used as part of the recreational activities during the Roman Saturnalia. As Sebo (2009, 34) points out, the collection "reveals that within Symphosius' milieu there is still a conception of riddles as oral and agonistic." As he (Sebo 2009, 36) goes on to remark, the riddles are more than simple guessing games; they indicate a new ludic-literary function, which endows them "with a new autonomy and intertextual sophistication." Autonomy from metaphysically based primary metaphors and connection to other tales about foxes (intertextuality) is what characterizes all situation-specific riddles.

Around a century later, the English scholar and poet Aldhelm (640–709 CE), produced a similar collection of a hundred riddles, also titled *Aenigmata*, adding to the rise of riddling as a ludic-literary verbal art (Juster 2015, 15). Aldhelm's riddles also focused on everyday things (animals, plants, household items, and so on). The following one, for example, is about a writing object (Aldhelm, *The Riddles of Aldhelm,* https://archive.org/details/riddlesofaldhelm0000aldh):

> I am bright white, born ages ago of the gleaming pelican
> Who takes the waters of the sea into his open mouth.
> Now I travel a narrow path over white-glowing fields
> I leave blue footprints along the shining way
> Obscuring bright fields with my blackened windings
> It is not enough for me to open one pathway through the fields
> Rather, the road runs its course in a thousand byways
> And leads those who stray not to the heights of Heaven.
> (*Answer:* a writing quill)

The fact that the riddle deals with writing suggests that literacy was becoming a requirement in medieval society. The metaphors in the riddle map referents that would have been concretely understandable to medieval people onto emerging writing and literacy concepts and objects—for instance, paper is portrayed as providing the "white-glowing fields," ink as leaving "blue footprints" and "blackened windings," in reference to written words, and so on. By mapping concrete, agricultural concepts onto writing implies that literacy allowed common folk to reach "the heights of Heaven," that is, to attain betterment in life, by allowing for understanding via the expression of thoughts or ideas in written form in some specific context of use.

Situation-specific riddles, such as these, are found throughout medieval societies, straddling literary and pedagogical functions, as can be seen conspicuously in the anonymous *Exeter Book* (c. 960 CE), also containing nearly a hundred riddles. As historical records suggest, these were likely intended for use in educating young people about the social meanings of everyday things by challenging them to think about them in metaphorical ways (Gameson 1996). Similarly, there is evidence that the riddles composed by English scholar Alcuin (c. 735–804 CE), who included them in his letter correspondences (Lapidge and Rosier 1985), were designed to get medieval people to think about the world they inhabited (discussed in chapter 2). In the tenth century, a number of Arabic scholars used riddles in an explicitly pedagogical way—to alert law students to the dangers that language, with all its ambiguities, double entendres, and semantic possibilities, poses for legal communication (Scott 1965). Al-Hariri of Basra (c. 1050–1120), for example, wrote a volume, titled *Assemblies*, containing riddles (Shah 1980) so as to illustrate to students of jurisprudence how misunderstandings in legal discourse can emerge via the play on words.

By the Renaissance, riddles were being tailored more and more to subserve an increasingly spreading secular leisure culture. In the eighteenth century, riddling had evolved into a literary genre all its own, generating a number of derivative types. Three of these—the *charade*, the *enigma*, and the *conundrum*—became highly popular especially in European society. The *charade* is solved by unraveling the various meanings suggested by playing with the separate syllables or letters in the required word or phrase that the riddle implies. The *enigma* contains one or more veiled references to the answer in the riddle statement itself. The *conundrum* is a term that covers various verbal twists, such as a riddle exploiting the similar sounds of word pairs or else involving a pun of some type. Below are examples of each type (to be discussed in more detail in the next chapter):

## Charade

(Lewis Carroll, *The Complete Works of Lewis Carroll*, Internet Archive: https://archive.org/details/completeworksofl1920carr)

> A monument—men all agree—Am I in all sincerity,
> Half cat, half hindrance made.
> If head and tail removed should be, then most of all you strengthen me;
> Replace my head, the stand you see
> On which my tail is laid.
> (*Answer*: a table)

This was composed by Lewis Carroll, which he published in his youthful journal *Mischmash*. The parts of the charade are as follows: "Half cat, half hindrance" = *tab-let*; "If head and tail removed" = that is, if the first and last letters of *tablet* are removed we get *able;* "Replace my head, the stand you see" = that is, put back the "t" in *able* to get *table*. The final line then describes the tabby cat's tail on the table (Williams, Madan, and Green 1962).

## Enigma

> We are little airy creatures, all of different voice and features.
> One of us in glass is set,
> One of us you'll find in jet.
> T'other you may see in tin,
> and the fourth a box within.
> If the fifth you should pursue,
> it can never fly from you.
> (*Answer*: A, E, I, O, U)

This was composed by English author Jonathan Swift, who was among the first to compose enigmas: "One of us in glass is set" = the vowel "A" is in the word *glass*; "One of us you'll find in jet"= the vowel E occurs in the word *jet*; "T'other you may see in tin" = the vowel I is found in in *tin*; "the fourth a box within" = the vowel O occurs in *box*; "If the fifth you should pursue" = the vowel U is found in *pursue*. Note that the riddle starts by describing the vowels correctly as "airy creatures," since they are articulated by emission of the air from the lungs with no obstruction as with the consonants, and that they are of "different voice and features."

## Conundrum

> Great bridges shall be made alone,
> Without ax, timber, earth or stone.
> Of chrystall metall, like to glass;
> Such wondrous works soon come to passe,
> If you may then have such a way.
> The Ferry-man you need not pay.
> (*Answer*: The cold)

This is from *An Almanack for the Year of Our Lord 1647* printed in Cambridge, Massachusetts by Samuel Danforth (1626–1674). It is a description of how the cold freezes water under bridges and how this can thus be used to avoid paying the "Ferry-man," since one can walk across frozen water.

These derivative riddling genres mirror how discourse itself had changed from antiquity to modernity, bringing "words back from their metaphysical to their everyday use," as Wittgenstein (1953, 116) put it. The mythic-metaphysical riddles, based on primary (root) metaphors, are the ones that are of specific interest for testing out the metaphor hypothesis. The subsequent functions of riddling are useful primarily in showing how they mirrored the evolution of the discourse functions of language. So, to evaluate the metaphor hypothesis, various collections of riddles from ancient societies are used as a philological database—including Rudolph (1942), Taylor (1948, 1951), Köngas-Maranda (1976), Dundes (1963), Georges and Dundes (1963), Senderovich (2005), Seyeb-Gohrab (2010), and Burrows (2014). Below is a chart summarizing the functions of riddles:

Of relevance to all phases, functions, and forms of riddling is the fact that language involves interpretation of the world—not just names for the different parts of the world. Each ancient riddle was a metaphysical interpretation of some phenomenon, event, or action, not just a chronological retelling of it. The seventeenth/eighteenth-century Italian philosopher Giambattista Vico (cited in Bergin and Fisch 1984) saw the original function of language as a means to convert the various images that the mind generates into verbal forms that are then used to interpret those very images reflectively; this might explain why the same kinds of metaphorical images are found in riddles and early myths across ancient societies. The evolution of riddling away from this metaphysical function to its other functions reflects how societies and discourse also developed (see Table 1.1). In later antiquity, riddles became especially popular as a pastime after dinners, such as wedding feasts—a tradition that is continued to this day in various cultures (Taylor 1951). The ancient Romans made riddles part of after-dinner activities at the Saturnalia, which they celebrated from December 17 to 23. This function extended well into the medieval period, with ludic riddle anthologies becoming broadly popular (as discussed above). By the later medieval period, riddles started appearing in narratives of all kinds, from fairy tales to nursery rhymes and entire works of fiction. For example, in the anonymous *100 Riddles of the Fairy Bellaria*,

**Table 1.1 Riddle Functions**

| Riddle Type | Function | Examples |
|---|---|---|
| Mythic | Riddles alluding to metaphysical concepts—based on primary (root) metaphors | Riddle of the Sphinx and other ancient riddles |
| Ludic | Riddles designed for recreation—created cleverly with situation-specific metaphors | The riddles of Symphosius, Aldhelm, and others |
| Literary | Riddles written in a poetic style, constituting a specific literary genre | Riddles such as charades, enigmas, and conundrums |
| Pedagogical | Riddles intended for training students in decoding the problems of language communication | The *Exeter Book*; the riddles of Al-Hariri of Basra |

published in 1892, a queen named Bellaria and her riddle-solving skills are pitted against a cruel invading king named Ruggero, who gives her a hundred riddles to solve. Ruggero threatens to destroy her empire should she fail to solve them successfully. The same utilization of riddling as a test of heroism appears in all kinds of narratives, such as *The Hobbit* (1937) and *Harry Potter and the Goblet of Fire* (2005), among many others. One of the first to incorporate riddles into children's literature was Lewis Carroll, who not only included actual riddles into his stories but designed the narrative themselves as overarching riddles (discussed in chapter 2).

Ludic riddles might also be the evolutionary source for verbal humor (Heesterman 1997). It is the developmental literature that can, again, be enlisted to give some substance to this hypothesis. As Paul McGhee (2002) has cogently argued (on the basis of the relevant literature), a kind of "riddle instinct" can be seen to emerge early on when five- to six-year-old children become interested in the puzzling questions of older children, who might give what seem like arbitrary answers that are followed by laughter. For example, the classic children's riddle, "Why did the chicken cross the road?" might involve answers that are humorous in intent, such as the following:

> To get to the other side.
> Because it was taken across by a farmer.
> Because a fox was chasing it.

All three state the obvious, but these might escape attention at first, provoking moderate laughter, similar to the kind that the "punch line" of jokes elicits (Wells 1988, 7). As McGhee goes on to remark, by the age of six or seven, children begin to understand the clever intent of riddles, discovering that the same word can have different meanings. At that point, children become consumed with riddles and tell them endlessly. Arguing retrospectively, it is not such a far-fetched assumption that when riddles entered the ludic stage, they might have concomitantly installed verbal humor as an emerging function of discourse. Certainly, there is no archeological-philological evidence of the emergence of the use of verbal humor before ludic riddling. While this may be a correlation rather than a causal link, there is little doubt that ludic riddles and humor are intertwined socially and cognitively (Kaivola-Bregenhøj 2017)—as both the ontogenetic and phylogenetic research strongly suggests.

## RIDDLES AND ROOT METAPHORS

The early mythic riddles, which were based on root metaphors, and the parallel myths that emerged at the same time are documents of how abstract culture might have coalesced from the metaphysical notions they enfolded (Jung 1959; Jaynes 1976). This is a key notion of the metaphor hypothesis, which is motivated by the appearance of root metaphorical concepts—*life is a journey, people are animals, objects are divine artifacts*, and so on—in both riddles and myths. As such, they constitute a philological field laboratory for testing out the relation among myth, metaphor, and the origin of language. They illustrate the uniquely human ability to "move to higher and higher levels of abstraction without limit," as Alfred Korzybski (1921) insightfully put it.

The mythic riddles emanate from a state of understanding and language that the Greeks called *mythos*, in contrast to *lógos*, exemplified instead by later riddling. The shift from *mythos* to *lógos* appears to be a principle of human cognitive evolution (Lévi-Strauss 1962; Eliade 1961). Aristotle was the one who coined the term *mythos* in his *Poetics* (Aristotle 1952b) to describe the plot structure of tragedies, which were connected in his era to the founding myths of Greek society (hence the term). *Mythos* can thus be seen to be the mindset underlying riddles and myths, while *lógos* underlies logical, rational argumentation (Hussey 1982). Socrates believed that *lógos* was innate in all human beings, teaching that individuals were born with it, and that it could be awakened through conscious reflection. However, Socrates did use irony in order to extract understanding from an interlocutor—a form of language that is hardly based in pure *lógos*.

A relevant interpretation of the *mythos*-versus-*lógos* distinction for the present purposes was put forth by the French sociologist Émile Durkheim (1912), who suggested that *mythos* allowed for the expression of a pattern of emotional responses to existence, thus constituting a certain form of wisdom that remains embedded in cultural memory (Durkheim 1912, 12), whereas *lógos* is a form of rational language that allows for the organization of cultural ideas. The anthropologist Bronislaw Malinowski (1922) also claimed that *mythos* provided an expressive means for coming to grips with the problems of reality that early people must have consciously confronted. He argued that, in its primitive form, mythic language was a way to grasp natural phenomena before the advent of science. Thus, the "thunder" in the sky was conceptualized as the angry voice of a god, "rain" as the weeping of the gods, and so on. From this, the names for *thunder* and *rain* were coined as divine words—for example, Thor in Norse mythology as the god of thunder and Mariamman as the Hindu goddess of rain. In Indo-European cultures, the thunder god is frequently conceptualized as the King of the Gods—for example, *Indra* in Hinduism, *Zeus* in Greek mythology, and *Perun* in ancient Slavic legend—indicating how primary metaphors undergirded the creation of the first abstract concepts, mapping natural phenomena such as the weather onto deistic figures, which were felt to govern the world from their metaphysical perches. As the Neapolitan philosopher Giambattista Vico insightfully observed, *Jove* (the god of the sky and thunder) was one of the first names devised by humans after becaming conscious of the thundering sky (Bergin and Fisch 1984, 374). Once this sky was called *Jove*, all other experiences of the same phenomenon were "found again" in this name.

Concepts such as the weather, time, and life were thus forged via root metaphors, appearing in myths and early riddles across the ancient world. For example, the *year unfolds like a wheel* metaphor has been found in riddles across antiquity. A Sanskrit riddle describes a "twelve-spoked wheel, on which stand 720 sons of one birth" alluding to the twelve months of the year, which together have 360 days and 360 nights (Tupper 1903, 102). Similarly, the *life phases* root metaphorical concept found in the Riddle of the Sphinx has been found in different cultures that could not have borrowed it from each other, given both the language barrier and the lack of cultural contacts. Below is an example from ancient Estonian (Aarne 1918):

It goes in the morning on four feet, at lunch-time on two, at evening on three.

Such riddles are clearly suggestive of the validity of the metaphor hypothesis, given that the ancient mythic riddles revealed the same pattern of conceptual metaphorical structure. Should a pattern of counterexamples to the hypothesis surface—that is, riddles based on widely differing metaphorical structures or perhaps even based on literal language—then the hypothesis would be disconfirmed. But the evidence in its favor is overwhelming as will be discussed throughout this book. Also, if the hypothesis is sustainable, then it should be the case that root metaphors, which are the founding structures of language, will have remained as unconscious patterns of thought, remaining not only in everyday language but also as part of subsequent riddle traditions. Two examples of the latter are Gollum's riddles in Tolkein's *The Hobbit* (1937, Internet Archive, https://archive.org/details/dli.ernet.474126):

> *Riddle 1:*
> What has roots as nobody sees,
> Is taller than trees,
> Up, up it goes,
> And yet never grows?
> (*Answer:* a mountain)
>
> *Riddle 2:*
> Voiceless it cries,
> Wingless flutters,
> Toothless bites,
> Mouthless mutters.
> (*Answer:* the wind)

The answer to both riddles involves two deeply embedded root metaphors. Riddle (1) portrays *mountains* as *plants* with invisible *roots* but which do not *grow*, thus mapping one domain of nature (*plants*) onto another *(mountains)* ontologically. Riddle (2) maps features of living things onto the *wind* (such as *crying, fluttering, biting*, and *muttering*) all of which are metaphors we use commonly in reference to the wind.

Actually, as such riddles show, a complementary function of root metaphors, in addition to encoding metaphysical concepts (*life unfolds like the phases of the day*), was the assignment of names to various phenomena (thunder, rain, and so on). This specific aspect of the metaphor hypothesis will be called *phenomenological*. The difference between *metaphysical* and *phenomenological* root metaphors is that the former involves such abstractions as the passage of time, while the latter involves naming them via the same metaphorical mechanism. Phenomenological metaphors are thus used to fill in lexical gaps in early referential systems—gaps left by concrete naming events. For example, lacking the name for the base of a mountain, the word *foot* was devised as a metaphor to fill in this gap. In effect, the early mythic riddles espoused two main cognitive functions—understanding metaphysical notions and naming phenomena that had not been named previously. This dichotomy is a useful one in testing the early riddles in terms of the metaphor hypothesis:

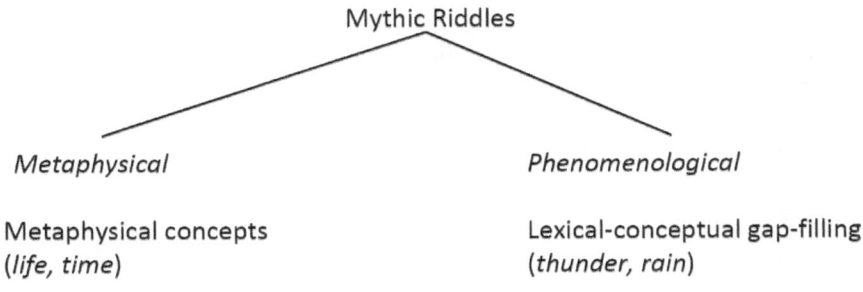

**Figure 1.1 A Mythic Riddle Dichotomy.**
Source: Marcel Danesi

## THE METAPHOR HYPOTHESIS

The metaphor hypothesis states that root metaphors are the source of language as a conceptual system, and these are found universally across ancient riddles and their attendant myths. It is based on the view of cognitive linguists that metaphor is a faculty of mind that produces understanding by connecting the realm of experience with abstract knowledge—a hypothesis first extensively discussed by George Lakoff and Mark Johnson in *Metaphors We Live By* (1980). Known broadly as *conceptual metaphor theory*, it has been investigated through psychological experiments, neuroscientific research, and anthropological investigations. The metaphor hypothesis applies the broader theory to the origins of language question, utilizing the earliest riddles and myths as putative philological evidence of the evolutionary shift from nominative speech to full-blown language via metaphor. This is an extraordinary claim, which requires substantive evidence to support it. So, it may be useful to schematically review the differing views of metaphor from antiquity to the present day as a backdrop to the motivation for considering metaphor as a faculty of the brain that produced the first true language-based artifacts.

It was Aristotle who discovered metaphor as a form of abstract understanding and as a gap-filler in the *Rhetoric* (1952a) and the *Poetics* (1952b), which he connects to riddles. In Book III of the former book (1952a, 123), he states that "good riddles do, in general, provide us with satisfactory metaphors: for metaphors imply riddles, and therefore a good riddle can furnish a good metaphor." However, Aristotle did not see metaphor as basic to ordinary language, considering literal speech to be its backbone, and metaphor as an attempt to expand literal speech into domains that it cannot possibly reach—hence, its ability to discover connections among things in the world. Leaving aside this dismissal, it is clear that the metaphor hypothesis traces its roots to Aristotle.

Aristotle also provided the first theory of metaphor, seeing it as a manifestation of proportional reasoning. For example, in the Sphinx's Riddle, the conceptualization of *old age* as *the evening of life* reveals the following proportion:

A = *old age*

B = *life*

C = *evening*

D = *day*

Therefore, A is to B as C is to D.

As Umberto Eco (1984, 88) pointed out, despite "the thousands and thousands of pages written about metaphor" since Aristotle formulated his theory, no novel explanation has ever really eclipsed it. Current conceptual metaphor theory (below) does not discard the Aristotelian view, but rather reformulates it simply as a cognitive mapping: *old age is the evening of life*. In both, the crux is that metaphor connects two domains of meaning that may at first seem unrelated; by so doing, it establishes the relation (by a proportion in the

Aristotelian model and by a mapping in the conceptual metaphor model). As Aristotle (1952b) put it, the ontological function of a riddle "is to express true facts under impossible combinations," thus producing unexpected knowledge (Aristotle 1952a):

> Well-constructed riddles are attractive [because] a new idea is conveyed. The thought is startled, and does not fit in with the ideas you already have. The effect produced is a surprise.

However, in the end Aristotle affirmed that the most common function of riddles was as a rhetorical strategy, emphasizing the need to use "clear diction" made up of "ordinary words," to carry out "familiar communication," avoiding the incomprehensible "jargon" that might otherwise emerge with the use of riddles (Aristotle 1952a, 34):

> The merit of diction is to be clear and not commonplace. The clearest diction is that made up of ordinary words, but it is commonplace. An example is the poetry of Cleophon and of Sthenelus. That which employs unfamiliar words is dignified and outside the common usage. By "unfamiliar" I mean a rare word, a metaphor, a lengthening, and anything beyond the ordinary use. But if a poet writes entirely in such words, the result will be either a riddle or jargon; if made up of metaphors, a riddle and if of rare words, jargon. The essence of a riddle consists in describing a fact by an impossible combination of words. By merely combining the ordinary names of things this cannot be done, but it is made possible by combining metaphors. For instance, "I saw a man weld bronze upon a man with fire," and so on. A medley of rare words is jargon. We need then a sort of mixture of the two. For the one kind will save the diction from being prosaic and commonplace, the rare word, for example, and the metaphor and the "ornament," whereas the ordinary words give clarity.

Roman rhetoricians subsequently modified the Aristotelian view by claiming that metaphor was a substitutive, decorative strategy, meant to enhance the meaning of something, not create it. Nevertheless, they too sensed a powerful cognitive force within its uses. In his *Institutio Oratoria*, Quintilian (1875), explained the use of *lion* in an utterance such as *Julius Caesar is a lion* as a rhetorical replacement of its literal counterpart, a *courageous man*, so as to make it more memorable and effective. Interestingly, in his *De Oratore*, Cicero (1942, 274) saw metaphor in seemingly modern-day terms, namely as the process of mapping sensory information against abstractions, thus providing the first implicit definition of a root conceptual metaphor:

> All metaphors, at least such of them that are best chosen, are applied to the senses, especially the seeing, which of all senses is the most exquisite. Thus when we say, the tincture of politeness, the softness of good-breeding, the

murmur of waters, and sweetness of language; these metaphors are all taken from the other senses. But the metaphors taken from the sense of seeing are much more striking, because they place in the eye of the imagination of objects ... otherwise ... impossible for us to see or comprehend. For there is nothing in nature but what we may adapt its name to signify something else; and every object from which a likeness may be raised, as it may from all objects, if metaphorically applied.

Discussions of metaphor remained largely dormant after antiquity—revived in the medieval period after Thomas Aquinas wrote in his *Summa Theologica* (1266–1273) that the writers of Holy Scripture presented "spiritual truths" under the "likeness of material things" because that was the only way in which humans could grasp such truths, thus implying that metaphor was a tool of cognition, not just a feature of rhetorical flourish (quoted in Davis and Hersh 1986, 250):

It is befitting Holy Scripture to put forward divine and spiritual truths by means of comparisons with material things. For God provides for everything according to the capacity of its nature. Now it is natural to man to attain to intellectual truths through sensible things, because all our knowledge originates from sense. Hence in Holy Scripture spiritual truths are fittingly taught under the likeness of material things.

But like those before him, Aquinas ultimately saw literal language as the core of conceptual knowledge, seeing the use of metaphor in sacred scripture as a means for humans to grasp divine truths. After Aquinas, philosophers continued largely to ignore, and even condemn, metaphor. The source of the latter view is, probably, John Locke's characterization of metaphor as a "fault" in his *Essay Concerning Humane Understanding* (Locke 1690, 34):

If we would speak of things as they are, we must allow that all the art of rhetoric, besides order and clearness, all the artificial and figurative application of words eloquence hath invented, are for nothing else but to insinuate wrong ideas, move the passions, and thereby mislead the judgment; and so indeed are perfect cheats: and therefore, however laudable or allowable oratory may render them in harangues and popular addresses, they are certainly, in all discourses that pretend to inform or instruct, wholly to be avoided; and where truth and knowledge are concerned, cannot but be thought a great fault, either of language or person that makes use of them.

Thomas Hobbes (1656) also inveighed fiercely against metaphor, characterizing it as an obstacle to communication, a source of ambiguity and obscurity, and thus, a feature of language to be eliminated from true philosophical and scientific discourse. Hobbes came to possess this view probably because he believed that the laws of arithmetic mirrored the laws of human thought, and thus that the only meaningful form of discourse was of the same kind as the one used to explicate mathematical notions.

It was Giambattista Vico (above) in the latter part of the seventeenth and early eighteenth centuries who provided one of the first theories of metaphor as intrinsic to language origins. He saw metaphor as the product of a universal sense-making capacity that he called *poetic logic* (Danesi 1993). In terms of the metaphor hypothesis, this can be defined as the form of mind that generated the first root metaphors which created what he called "fables in brief," which today would be called conceptual metaphors (Vico in Bergin and Fisch 1984, 404):

> All the first tropes are corollaries of this poetic logic. The most luminous and therefore the most necessary and frequent is metaphor. It is most praised when it gives sense and passion to insensate things, in accordance with the metaphysics above discussed, by which the first poets attributed to bodies the being of animate substances, with capacities measured by their own, namely sense and passion, and in this way made fables of them. Thus every metaphor so formed is a fable in brief.

Poetic logic will be discussed in detail in chapter 3. Suffice it to say here that Vico's view that metaphor was evidence of how the human mind produces the first concepts (fables) went largely unnoticed, although the power of metaphor to shape thinking did start to attract some notice. For example, Immanuel Kant suggested in his *Critique of Pure Reason* (Kant 1790) that metaphor made unfamiliar things understandable. Friedrich Nietzsche (1873) even suggested that metaphor was humanity's greatest flaw, because of its unconscious power to persuade people into believing it on its own terms. For Nietzsche it is thus the source of our superstitions and of unfounded belief systems, along with other kinds of figurative strategies (Nietzsche 1873, 23):

> What then is truth? A movable host of metaphors, metonymies, and anthropomorphisms: in short, a sum of human relations which have been poetically and rhetorically intensified, transferred, and embellished, and which, after long usage, seem to a people to be fixed, canonical, and binding. Truths are illusions which we have forgotten are illusions—they are metaphors that have become worn out and have been drained of sensuous force, coins which have lost their embossing and are now considered as metal and no longer as coins.

It was around the same time that the debate concerning literal-versus-metaphorical meaning started to coalesce, becoming a major one in the late twentieth century (summarized in detail by Lakoff 1986). Literal language has concrete referential functions—a function of early speech (as will be discussed). So, when a word such as *cat* is used in an utterance such as *The cat is on the mat*, its meaning is literal. But even in this case, there is much more packed into the sentence than straightforward denotative reference to a scene involving a cat and a mat, such as as the likelihood that the cat is in a home, that it is an animal companion, and so on. While these inferences are not strictly tied to metaphor, they nonetheless show that any word, even if used literally, generates images that transcend its pure literal referential meaning.

The problem with literalist theories is that they consider the meanings of words in isolation. In an expression such as *candy is sweet* we can easily detach *sweet* from the phrase and define it literally as "having a pleasant taste." It is when the word is combined with an abstraction such as *love*—*love is sweet*—that metaphorical suggestiveness comes into focus. This expression implies that *love* and *sweetness* implicate each other—as in *She's my sweetheart*; *I love my honey*; and so on. Moreover, the metaphorical expression is a key to understanding why chocolates are given to a loved one on Valentine's Day, love is ritualized at a wedding ceremony by the eating of a cake, and so on. This suggests an interrelationship between culture and metaphor. The root metaphor here is that of *love as nourishing food*. This comes out even more concretely in Chagga, a Bantu society of Tanzania, where the male in courtship situations is conceived as an *eater* and the female as his *sweet food*, as can be detected in expressions that mean, in translated form, *Does she taste sweet? She tastes sweet as sugar honey* (Emantian 1995). These are not exceptions; they are the rule, substantiating the metaphor hypothesis at various levels including the cultural one. They also suggest that metaphorical interpretation is not an option. If contextual information is missing from an utterance such as *The murderer is an animal*, our inclination is to interpret it metaphorically, not literally. It is only if we are told that the *murderer* is an actual "animal" (a bear, a cougar, and so on) that a literal interpretation comes into focus.

Scientific interest in the literal versus metaphor distinction started in early experimental psychology in the latter part of the nineteenth century and the early twentieth. One of the founders—the German linguist-physiologist Wilhelm Wundt (1901)—conducted experiments on how people processed figurative language. Karl Bühler (1908) followed suit, collecting intriguing data on how subjects paraphrased and recalled proverbs. He found that the recall of a given proverb was statistically higher if it was linked to a second proverb. Bühler concluded that metaphorical-connective thinking produced an effective retrieval form of memory and was, therefore, something to be investigated further in contrast to literal recall. Shortly after, the Gestalt movement emerged to make the study of metaphor a primary target of research. Solomon Asch (1950), for instance, examined metaphors of sensation (*hot, cold, heavy*, and so on) in several unrelated languages as descriptors of emotional states. He found that *hot* stood for *rage* in Hebrew, *enthusiasm* in Chinese, *sexual arousal* in Thai, and *energy* in Hausa (a language spoken in northern Nigeria, Niger, and adjacent areas). This suggested to him that, while the specific emotion implicated varied from language to language, the metaphorical process did not. Simply put, people seemed to think of emotions in terms of physical sensations and expressed them as such. As Roger Brown (1958, 146) commented shortly after the publication of Asch's findings, there is "an undoubted kinship of meanings" in different languages that "seem to involve activity and emotional arousal"; and that this "kinship" is revealed through metaphor.

The scholar who developed the first true cognitive model of metaphor several years earlier, called *interactionist*, was I. A. Richards in his groundbreaking book *The Philosophy of Rhetoric* (1936). The meaning inherent in, say, the Shakespearean metaphor "all the world's a stage" (from *As You Like It*, II:7:139) there is a conceptual interaction between *life* (*the world*) and *stages*, with one implying the other: the implication is that what happens on a stage is an imitation of life, and that life is perceived to unfold as if it were on a stage. Richards was the first to label the parts of the metaphor as follows: (1) the metaphorical concept itself is the *tenor* or *topic* (*life*); (2) the notion to which it is linked is the *vehicle* (a *stage*); and (3) the meaning produced by the linkage is the *ground (life is a stage = stages represent life)*. As a case in point of how this would explain a common metaphor, consider *John is a gorilla*. The topic in this case is a person named *John* and the vehicle is the animal termed a *gorilla*. Portraying *John* as a *gorilla* implies that the two are alike in some way—hence the ground, which is the image of a person with gorilla-like characteristics or, vice versa, the image of a gorilla with human-like qualities. One image blends into the other. But this blending would not occur if the topic and vehicle were not perceived as exemplars of each other in the first place. This suggests a different more general level of metaphor. Changing the vehicle brings this out clearly. If one were to label *John* as a *snake*, a *weasel*, or a *puppy*, rather than a *gorilla*, then our image of *John* would change in kind with each new vehicle—he would become snake-like, weasel-like, and puppy-like in our minds. This suggests that all such metaphors are instances of a general-level metaphor—namely, *people are animals* or in reverse, *animals are people*. This idea of a general level was subsequently discussed by Max Black (1962), who argued that the two categories—*people* and *animals*—are linked to each other because they are perceived to be subcategories of each other. So, the area of interaction between these two is the conceptual ground that is produced by the linkage:

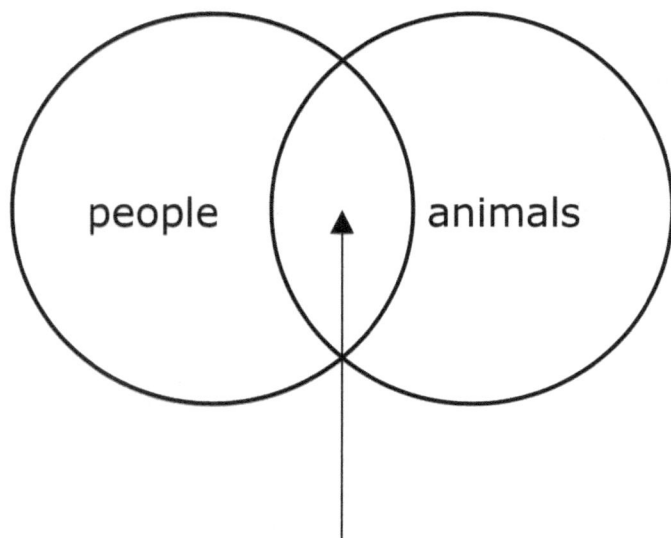

*[People are animals – Animals are people]*

**Figure 1.2 Interactionist Model of Metaphor.**
Source: Marcel Danesi

The name given by Lakoff (1979) a little later to the general metaphorical structure is *conceptual metaphor*. This implies that each particular *linguistic metaphor* (*John is a gorilla, John is a snake*, and so on) is not an isolated example of poetic fancy, but rather a token of an abstract typological metaphor. As an aside, it is noteworthy that the same conceptual metaphor is found in many early riddles, implying that it is a root metaphor. The fox riddle above is one such example of *animals are people*. Given that the same concept is found in riddles and myths throughout antiquity, it can be established as a universal output of the metaphorical mind. Even the mythological sphinxes are products of the same metaphorical conceptualization, giving the concept a visual form.

The approach above raises a fundamental question: Can any vehicle be linked to any topic to produce a ground? Seemingly, the very act of linkage invariably impels the mind to assign a meaning-ground to it, no matter how unfamiliar or strange the result may appear (Honeck and Hoffman 1980). For example, the phrase *Love is a pine nut* might seem bizarre at first, but upon further consideration one can start to see a connection such as the property of taste that *love* and *pine nuts* share (*love* through oscular contact and *pine nuts* through mastication). As unlikely as this is at a literal level of understanding, we nonetheless grasp what the metaphor is attempting to achieve—a connection between two domains of meaning on the basis of a shared property. This is strong indirect evidence in support of the premise that metaphor is at the root of conceptual language. Another question is this: Does the interaction between the two parts of a metaphor necessarily involve a concrete (vehicle)-to-abstract (topic) process? There are metaphors where this is not the case. For example, *Love is sublime* involves an abstract topic (*love*) and an abstract vehicle (*sublimity*). This means that there are different levels or layers of metaphor (as will be discussed subsequently). However, it is the root level that is of primary interest in testing the metaphor hypothesis. At this primary level, the concrete-to-abstract process is the one that manifests itself across the early riddles.

Research on conceptual metaphor theory has made the literal versus metaphor debate essentially a moot one, despite some critiques that need not concern us here, since they have been largely answered in the metaphor research literature (for an overview see Gibbs 2017). Starting with Black (1962), even scientists are coming to the conclusion that their theories have an underlying metaphorical genesis. The philosopher of science, Fernand Hallyn (1990), has even identified the goal of science as that of giving the world a "poetic structure," recalling Vico (above). As an example of such structure, it was first speculated that atomic structure mirrors the solar system, which is a clear metaphorical guess. It is mind-boggling to think that such a simple conceptual linkage has led to real knowledge about atoms. Physicists have never seen the inside of an atom with their eyes. So, they have used their inner metaphorical eye to produce a hunch about what an atom looks like, with electrons orbiting around an atomic nucleus like the planets orbit a star. As Max Black (1962) pointed out, this became a scientific model that led to a whole spate of experimental research and discoveries that now fall under the rubric of quantum physics.

Physicists no longer use this simple metaphor, but without it they never would have come up with the ideas that they have developed over time. It is metaphor that renders visible in the imagination those things we cannot literally see with our eyes—atoms, sound waves, gravitational forces, magnetic fields, and so forth. This is why sound waves are said to *undulate* through empty space like water waves ripple through a still pond; atoms to *leap* from one quantum state to another; electrons to *travel in circles* around an atomic nucleus; and so on. The physicist K. C. Cole (1985, 156) puts it as follows:

> The words we use are metaphors; they are models fashioned from familiar ingredients and nurtured with the help of fertile imaginations. "When a physicist says an electron is like a particle," writes physics professor Douglas Giancoli, "he is making a metaphorical comparison like the poet who says "love is like a rose." In both images a concrete object, a rose or a particle, is used to illuminate an abstract idea, love or electron.

As will be discussed in chapter 3, metaphors in all domains of knowledge provide "inner vision." As Jean Baudrillard (1987, 7) aptly put it, "Everywhere one seeks to produce meaning, to make the world signify, to render it visible."

## CONCEPTUAL METAPHOR THEORY

The metaphor hypothesis was given some empirical validation by a 1977 study that showed that metaphor pervades common everyday speech. A team of research psychologists headed by Howard Pollio found that speakers of English uttered, on average, an astounding three thousand novel metaphors and seven thousand idioms (dead metaphors) per week. The study made it obvious that metaphor could hardly be construed as a deviation from literal language or a mere stylistic option to it. This was followed by a key 1979 collection of studies compiled by Andrew Ortony, *Metaphor and Thought*, the 1980 anthology put together by Richard P. Honeck and Robert R. Hoffman, *Cognition and Figurative Language*, and the 1980 book by George Lakoff and Mark Johnson, *Metaphors We Live By*. All these laid the groundwork for conceptual metaphor theory to be fashioned.

It is this theory of metaphor that can be seen to have implications for the study of riddles, since they are implanted on root conceptual metaphors, such as *life unfolds as the phases of a day*. It is useful, therefore, to provide a schematic synopsis of conceptual metaphor theory. In the *phases* conceptual metaphor, *life* is the target domain and *parts of a day* are the *source domain*. The latter is mapped onto the former via the perception of *time* as consisting of sequential events or phases. Once formed, this becomes an unconscious guide to understanding both *life* and *time*. The concept of *mapping* is key to the theory, since it implies that parts of the brain are enlisted to understand concepts in other parts. Starting in 2002, with the work of Gilles Fauconnier and Mark Turner, the mapping is said to produce a *blend* (which is largely equivalent to the original *ground* of interaction theory). In the Riddle of the Sphinx, the *phases of the day* are mapped onto *life* and vice versa, producing the blend. This process is different from analogy, which is an intentional comparison devised to make something understandable, whereas metaphorical mapping is largely unconscious. The difference, as Vico also understood, is that metaphor as an "isness" process, whereas analogy is a "likeness" process (Verene 1981). In metaphor there is a perception that things *are* connected in some way; in analogy, the strategy is to make connections in order to clarify something.

An interesting and relevant finding of conceptual metaphor research concerns so-called nonsense or anomalous strings. It was Noam Chomsky (1957) who first used such strings—for example, *Colorless green ideas sleep furiously*—to argue that the syntactic rules of a language were independent from semantics. Such strings have the "feel" of real sentences because they consist of real English words put together in a syntactically appropriate fashion. This forces us to interpret the string as legitimate, but meaningless—a fact which suggests that we process meaning separately from syntax. What Chomsky ignored was that although we do not extract literal meaning from such strings, we are invariably inclined to extract a metaphorical meaning from them (Pollio and Burns 1977; Pollio and Smith 1979; Connor and Kogan 1980). This suggests that we are inclined to glean metaphorical meaning from any well-formed string of words, and that literal meaning is probably the exception. As Winner (1982, 253) aptly put it, if "people were limited to strictly literal language, communication would be severely curtailed, if not terminated."

Empirical evidence supporting the premise that metaphor is a faculty of mind is abundant (for example, Gibbs 2017 and Kövecses 2020). However, if this claim is to be given historical validation, then examining the earliest philologically available linguistic artifacts, such as the ancient riddles, is clearly relevant. As an initial attempt at enlisting such evidence, consider the small sample of ancient riddles, labeled according to their conceptual metaphorical structure (Taylor 1948, 1951; Salomon 1996; Kaivola-Bregenhøj 2016). These and others will be examined in more detail in chapter 4:

**Table 1.2 Riddles and Conceptual Metaphor Theory**

| Riddle | Answer | Origin | Conceptual Metaphor |
|---|---|---|---|
| There is a house. One enters it blind and comes out seeing. What is it? | A school house | Sumerian cuneiform tablet | *Target*: knowledge *Source*: seeing, vision, school buildings = structures that "contain" knowledge |
| What becomes pregnant without conceiving and large without eating? | A rain cloud | Babylonian tablet | *Target*: rain *Source*: pregnant stomach |
| It is a twelve-spoked wheel, on which stand 720 sons of one birth. | A calendar year | Sanskrit manuscript | *Target*: year as a time construct *Sources*: wheel = the year as a recurring cycle; twelve spokes = 12 months; 720 sons of one birth = 360 days and 360 nights |
| Bunched up behind the hummock, curled up under a stone, a disc at the foot of a stump. | A snake | Finnish folklore | *Target*: snake *Source*: disc shape when curled referring to the nature of snakes themselves |

When the range of ancient riddle traditions is further enlarged, what emerges is the same pattern of source domains (wheels, family members, animal shapes, and so on) across languages that are mapped against the same kinds of target domains (knowledge, time, animals, and so on). This type of riddle database thus provides philological evidence upon which to assert the validity of the metaphor hypothesis, as will be discussed throughout this book.

Lakoff and Johnson posited that the linkage between source and target domains was realized via the mental mechanism of *image schemas* (Lakoff 1987; Johnson 1987; Lakoff and Johnson 1999). These are mental impressions of sensory, affective, or culturally guided experiences that the brain schematizes and then maps onto various other areas or spaces. For example, an image schema derived from the physical experience of orientation and distance—*up* vs. *down, back* vs. *front, near* vs. *far*, and so on—manifests itself regularly in metaphorical expressions related to mood (*Life is looking up today*, *There is no need to feel down*), achievement (*She has reached the top of her field*, *Success is near*), and so on. So, source domains such as *phases, journeys, buildings, wheels, body parts, celestial bodies, food, seeing*, among others, revolve ultimately around the need to understand life in concrete ways through a clustering of image schemas. The clustering can be shown as follows:

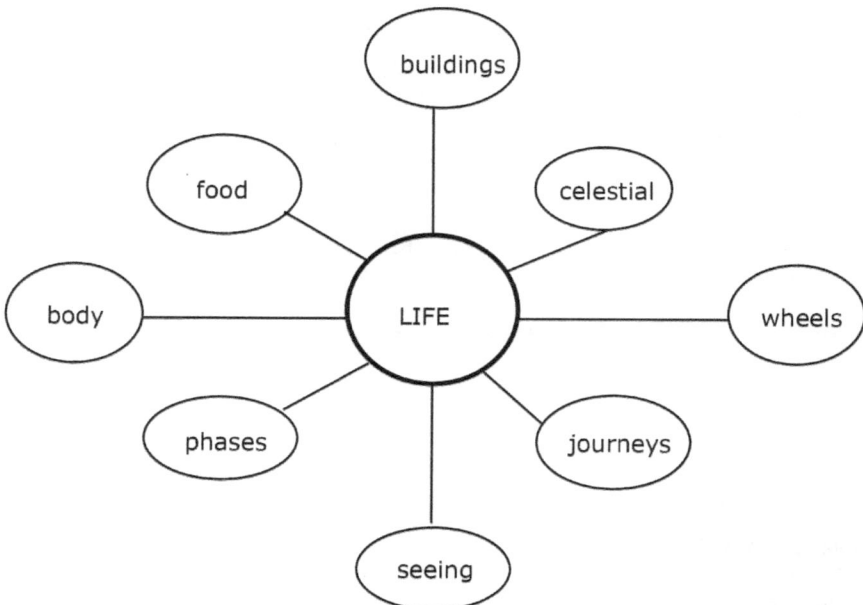

**Figure 1.3 Metaphorical Clustering.**
*Source:* Marcel Danesi

The source domains above are relatively understandable across cultures: that is, people from non-English-speaking cultures could easily figure out what metaphors based on these domains mean if they were translated or relayed to them. The reason is that they are based on root metaphors. Source domains that are situation-specific (above), such as, for instance, the use of *geometrical figures* for *ideas* (*I see your point*, *Our ideas are diametrically opposite*, *That idea is a circular one*, and so on) may be beyond easy cross-cultural comprehension, especially in those cultures where Euclidean geometry is not part of its cultural image schematic system.

As mentioned in the introduction, it was Eve Sweetser (1990) who first presented solid philological evidence to suggest that some image schemas are the source of abstract words and expressions, which have been called phenomenological metaphors in this book. For some reason, her line of research was not pursued in any systematic way. As Sweetser showed, expressions such as *behold* and *catch sight of* are manifestations of conceptual metaphors that implicate abstract image schemas based on manual capacities and vision, *examine* is from Latin *ex* + *agmen* "to pull out from a row," *speculate* derives from Latin *speculari* "to look at," Hebrew *litpos* "to grasp" is used to mean "to understand," Maori *kura* "seeing" refers to "knowledge in general," Japanese *yoin* "reverberating sound" designates "human feelings," and so on. As Walter Ong (1977, 134) has aptly remarked, the apparent universality of such source domains suggests that "we would be incapacitated for dealing with knowledge and intellection without massive visualist conceptualization." The image schematic link between hands and vision produces metaphors of *ideas* such as *look at, touch, hold, take apart, see*, and so on (*Take a close look at this new theory*, *It has touched upon several key issues*, *It does not hold together since it can be easily taken apart*, and so on). Not all the early abstract thoughts were forged in this way. The word *contemplate* derives from Latin *templum* "temple," and the word *mind* has referred exclusively to abstract thinking for at least five thousand years (Wescott 1980, 27). But, by and large, abstract concepts are the result of a metaphorical mappings that project sensory perceptions and physical experiences onto abstractions.

Clearly, the metaphor hypothesis can be enlisted to validate conceptual metaphor theory at a root formation level of language. It can also be applied to proverbial language, which, like riddles and myths, is intrinsic to early folkloric culture. A common expression such as *He has fallen from grace* would have been interpreted instantly in previous eras as referring to the Genesis story in the Bible. Today we continue to use it with only a dim awareness (if any) of its Biblical origins. Expressions that portray *life as a journey*—*I'm still a long way from my goal*, *There is no end in sight*, and so on—are found in all kinds of early verbal artifacts, from riddles and myths to proverbs. As the Canadian literary critic Northrop Frye (1990) aptly pointed out, one cannot penetrate such expressions, and indeed most of Western history, without having been exposed, directly or indirectly, to the original image schemas, which bestow a kind of implicit metaphysical meaning and value to everyday life. As the small sample below illustrates, the target domain in proverbial language is *advice* and the source domains that are enlisted involve a concrete experience of things:

| | |
|---|---|
| *Proverb*: | You've got too many fires burning |
| *Target*: | advice to not do so many things at once |
| *Source*: | fire is beyond human control |
| | |
| *Proverb*: | Rome wasn't built in a day |
| *Target*: | advice to have patience |
| *Source*: | building something important takes time |
| | |
| *Proverb*: | Don't count your chickens before they're hatched |
| *Target*: | advice to be cautious |
| *Source*: | egg hatching as a source of life (new things) |
| | |
| *Proverb*: | An eye for an eye and a tooth for a tooth |
| *Target*: | vindication |
| *Source*: | body parts as essential to human life |

It should be mentioned that there are two other tropes that are part of conceptual metaphor theory, considered separately from metaphor—metonymy and irony. This distinction is relevant to the description of the subsequent discourse functions of riddling (ludic, pedagogical, literary). In this model of discourse, metonymy is using the name of one element in a source domain that is associated with the target (for example, *the White House* for *the President*). Generally, irony is a kind of incongruous mapping for emphasis. If a choreographer stated *You were very graceful!* so that dancers would become aware of their awkward moves, then it is understood as irony—a mapping of *graceful* onto *dancing* when the reverse is intended (*lack of grace*). In essence, incongruity is the core of irony. In the Oedipus legend, Oedipus kills a man on his way to Thebes to unravel the mystery of his fate as predicted by the oracle. He does not know that the man is Laius, his father. When he becomes the King of Thebes, he is told that someone had slain the previous king, Laius. Oedipus thus puts a curse on the slayer of Laius. The irony is that Oedipus has unknowingly cursed himself.

## THE LANGUAGE ORIGINS QUESTION

The metaphor hypothesis makes the claim that language originated as a shift from nomination to conceptualization. The indirect evidence for this shift comes from the developmental research, since it appears when children start employing the names for things that they had already acquired to form complex thoughts via metaphor (Vygotsky 1962). For the sake of argument, the term *speech* in this book is restricted to designate the nominative function of words or manual gestures, as it manifests itself in infancy and by retroactive argument in the first speech forms. Of course, as it is defined today, speech is a much broader concept, often equated with *discourse*. The term *language* is used instead to designate the use of words in some combinatory fashion to express complex thoughts.

The first comprehensive modern-day treatment of the origins question is Danish linguist Otto Jespersen's *Language, Its Nature, Development and Origin* (1922). In the book, Jespersen identified "echoism" as the major factor producing the first words—a view that can be traced to the ancient Greeks (Stam 1976). The basic idea in echoism (called *iconicity* in current linguistics and semiotics) is that the imitation of natural sounds is the stimulus behind the creation of the first words via the vocal apparatus. Stross (1976, 21) describes echoism as follows:

> Humans and birds especially seem to have rather well developed abilities to imitate many environmental sounds, especially sounds made by other animals, and this ability could well have been very useful to protohominids for luring game. Could sounds used by protohominids to lure game or mimic sounds of nature come to represent the game or other objects in nature in the minds of these prelinguistic humans?

Echoism might indeed explain how the first names for things were devised, as will be discussed further in Chapter 5. Thousands of words in reconstructed languages such as Proto-Indo-European (PIE) and Nostratic show that it is a constant pattern in the coinage of the first forms of speech (Ross 1991; Bomhard 1992). Aided by statistical analysis and computer technology today, linguists can now establish phonetic patterns among early core vocabularies (Gamkrelidze and Ivanov 1990; Gray and Atkinson 2003; Currie, Meade, Guillon, and Mace 2013). Such vocabularies have established an "echoic" relation between the nature of speech sounds and the meanings they encode—a relation called *sound symbolism* (to be discussed further in Chapter 5). For instance, the reconstructed PIE word for "ox" is *$k^w ou$ (Gamkrelidze and Ivanov 1990, 113), which can be seen to be imitative of the sound that an ox might be perceived as making by early human speakers. A few other examples in PIE and Nostratic are given in Table 1.3 (Swadesh 1951, 1959, 1971; Gamkrelidze and Ivanov 1990, 114–115):

Table 1.3 Reconstructed Words

| Word | Language | Echoic-Iconic Features |
| --- | --- | --- |
| yotor "water" | PIE | /y/-/r/ = imitative of liquid sounds |
| ekhos "horse" | PIE | /kʰ/ = expiratory sound that a horse might make |
| woi-no "grape" | PIE | /woy/ = squeezing sound such as that made by grapes |
| klak "laugh" | PIE | /klak/ = chuckling sound |
| pek "to fleece" | PIE | /p/-/k/ = sound resembling the sound of shearing sheep |
| bhegu- "to flee" | PIE | /bʰ/-/gᵘ/ = imitative of effortful sounds expended while fleeing |
| keu- "to hear" | PIE | /k/-/u/ = imitative of expiration sounds that accompany the emphatic articulation of words |
| bhreg- "to break" | PIE | /bʰ/-/g/ = sounds suggestive of the action of breaking things |
| ghed- "to take" | PIE | /gʰ/ = sound suggestive of the action of grabbing something swiftly |
| kküyna "wolf, dog" | Nostratic | /kküy/ = imitative of wolf and dog howling |
| lapa "leaf" | Nostratic | /l/- /p/ = imitative of sounds made when touching a leaf |
| chunga "odor" | Nostratic | /tʃ/-/ga/ = responsive sound to odor, like a sneeze, made when air is expelled through the nasal canal |

One of the earliest theories connecting echoic speech with language via metaphor was formulated by the eighteenth-century philosopher Jean Jacques Rousseau (1966). Rousseau proposed that the natural cries that early humans must have shared with the animals, and the gestures that they used in tandem, led to the invention of vocal speech. He explained the evolutionary transition in this way: when the gestures proved to be too cumbersome, their corresponding cries replaced them. Rousseau also proposed what certainly must have been a radical idea for his era—that metaphor was a cognitive remnant of a previous, and hence more fundamental, stage in the evolution of the mind. Rousseau considered the first metaphorical utterances to be the mental counterparts of physical gestures (Rousseau 1966, 12):

> As man's first motions for speaking were of the passions, his first expressions were tropes. Figurative language was the first to be born. Proper meaning was discovered last. One calls things by their true name only when one sees them in their true form. At first only poetry was spoken; there was no hint of reasoning until much later.

In the early part of the twentieth century, Richard Paget (1930) gave a similar explanation of a plausible gesture-to-vocal speech process, claiming that manual gestures were copied unconsciously by positions and movements of the lips and tongue. Their continual apposition led eventually to the replacement of the former by the latter (Paget 1930, 24):

> Human speech arose out of a generalized unconscious pantomimic gesture language—made by the limbs as a whole (including the tongue and lips)—which became specialized in gestures of the organs of articulation, owing to the hands becoming continually occupied with the use of tools. The gestures of the organs of articulation were recognized by the hearer because the hearer unconsciously reproduced in his mind the actual gesture which had produced the sound.

Such theories have been shown to be compatible with brain and vocal tract evolution (Hewes 1973, 1976). But there is no indication in the relevant research of the role of metaphor as the mechanism initiating the shift from vocal speech to conceptual language. In a specific way, the metaphor hypothesis extends Rousseau's description so as to suggest that the transition occurred via conceptual metaphors and that the evidence for this is to be found in the early riddles, myths, and other forms of folkloric speech.

## EPILOGUE

A theory of the origins of language via an analysis of the source domains and image schemas of early riddles and myths implies that they emanate from a shared experience of reality that is lodged in the collective unconscious of humanity, as Jung (1959) and others have called it. The fact that similar riddle traditions, with virtually identical source domains, exist across the world, regardless of language, suggests that their metaphorical structure is intrinsic to human consciousness.

Most of the root metaphors found in riddles originated in tandem with a culture's myths, which are the founding narratives of a culture (Eliade 1961). The Zuñi people of North America, for instance, claim to have emerged from a mystical hole in the earth, thus establishing their kinship metaphorically with the land; Rome was said to have been founded by Romulus, who as an infant had to be suckled by a wolf, thus alluding to a certain animal fierceness of the Roman people; and so on. Myths create a metaphysical knowledge system for explaining human origins, actions, and character. Riddles are condensed myths themselves, designed to allow people to grasp existential-metaphysical notions concretely.

As mentioned at the start of this chapter, the metaphor hypothesis is consistent with the idea that "ontogeny recapitulates phylogeny," formulated in the nineteenth century, given that the appearance of metaphor in childhood likely recapitulates the transition from early nominative speech to full-blown language (Gould 1977). As Milner (1990, 44) has remarked, during that century it "was considered one of the proofs of evolution." In the twentieth century, the Russian psychologist Lev Vygotsky's (1962) work on childhood development provided indirect support for the metaphor hypothesis. As he (1962, 298) put it, "The primary word is not a straightforward symbol for a concept but rather an image, a picture, a mental sketch of a short concept, a short tale about it—indeed, a small work of art." When viewed cumulatively, the developmental literature suggests that it would not be farfetched to compare the child's first concepts to those of early makers of riddles.

*Chapter Two*

# Riddle Functions

**PROLOGUE**

The word *riddle* derives from Old English *rædels*, basically meaning "opinion." As far as can be told, languages of the world have lexical equivalents—in Italian it is *indovinello*, in Croatian it is *zagonetka*, in Finnish *arvoitus*, in Turkish *bilmece*, and so on. In Greek antiquity, the word for riddle was *aenigma*, which meant "obscure speech." The Greeks also coined the word *griphos* to designate a humorous question with a nonobvious answer, thus distinguishing between abstract riddles and riddle jokes (later called conundrums). A modern example is the following:

> Where does an elephant go when it wants to lie down?
> (*Answer:* Anywhere it can).

As a riddle joke it is both humorous and surprising because the question seems to concern the habits of elephants, but it ends up being about the large size of elephants and the problem of finding a resting place for such a bulky corporeal mass.

As the early mythic riddles embedded themselves into language and thought via conceptual metaphors, riddles started taking on new functions, leading to ludic, literary, and pedagogical traditions based on riddles, as discussed in the previous chapter. Originally part of folk wisdom, riddles developed subsequent discourse functions, including the strategic deployment of humor as a commentary on life. As Dutch historian Johan Huizinga (1938) emphasized, the ludic instinct, physical and intellectual, is undervalued as a factor in the foundation of institutionalized culture, as evidenced indirectly by the common fact that, at an unconscious level, people seemingly perceive life, or aspects of life, as a kind of ongoing game—borne out by many situation-specific (and thus language-specific) metaphors (*You must play by the rules*, *There is no winning or losing in life*, *Life is a series of chess moves*, etc.). The emergence of the ludic, literary, and pedagogical functions of riddling actually started in antiquity (appearing a little later than the mythic riddles), as can be seen in fables such as those of Aesop, which served early discourse functions. By the medieval period these became dominant in riddling traditions and uses. As Erin Sebo's (2009) work has shown, medieval riddles were framed with a high poetic quality transforming riddling into a literary art and a new speech form. The overriding function of all types of riddles is to interpret reality, or cast imaginative light on it, rather than just refer to it. This is arguably why riddles are intrinsically intertwined with the original myths, legends, and folkloric traditions of ancient societies. The early mythic riddles also had a social function—divination—as exemplified by the fact that they were the language of the ancient oracles—such as the one at Delphi who was the one who had pronounced Oedipus's fate.

This chapter will deal with the various functions of riddles—understanding, delectation, literary expression, and pedagogy. There are few records of ancient uses of language other than riddles, which can thus be used as materials for testing the metaphor hypothesis (in subsequent chapters). As Hovanec (1978, 12) aptly remarks,

> Riddles would have to be considered the oldest form of puzzles. They are to be found throughout the mythologies of many cultures and were important in ancient religion and philosophy as one of the vehicles through which the sages expressed their wisdom. Primitive peoples were obsessed with imagery and looked upon the ability to pose and solve riddles as indicative of mental agility.

To reiterate here, the early riddles provide philological data suggesting how nominative speech evolved into language and then how they evolved to undergird many of the discourse functions of language. The flow from naming to complex thinking via metaphor is the crux of the metaphor hypothesis, which is elaborated further in this chapter.

## UNDERSTANDING

As mentioned in chapter 1, the Riddle of the Sphinx emerged long before Sophocles's play *Oedipus Rex*, where it is alluded to, rather than stated explicitly. It reflects the metaphysical function of early riddles prototypically, illustrating dramatically how the first abstract notions were portrayed via metaphor. Similar riddles have been found inscribed on tablets, dating back to 2000 BCE and before (Seyeb-Gohrab 2010, 14). Some of the oldest surviving mythic riddles are those in the Sanskrit *Rigveda* and various other Vedic texts (Taylor 1948; Salomon 1996). In these sources, a fascination with the riddle form itself as a source of understanding things can be detected, not unlike how the word *riddle* is used in everyday English discourse—the *riddle of life,* the *riddle of the universe,* the *riddle of language,* and so on—revealing a view of riddles as a means for *understanding* things that are beyond the senses.

Talking about understanding shows how we conceptualize it, since it revolves around root source domains (seeing, touching, hearing):

> I cannot quite grasp what this is all about.
> *Source domain*: touch
> I do not see the reason for this.
> *Source domain*: vision
> Do you hear what I am saying?
> *Source domain*: hearing

Aware of this problem, Ludwig Wittgenstein (1969) looked past a definition of *understanding* focusing instead on what implications could be derived by examining the words used to achieve it. So, understanding an abstraction such as *life* is achieved via root metaphors, such as the ones above. In effect, *understanding* can only be understood metaphorically, not literally.

The Riddle of the Sphinx is one of the first, if not *the* first, example of how metaphor subserves understanding via riddling and how it is interconnected with narrative thinking—in this case, the myth of Oedipus. A version of the story goes as follows. The baby Oedipus was born to the Theban king Laius and his wife Jocasta. Laius consulted the Oracle at Delphi about the birth; the Oracle tells him that he will be killed by his own son, Oedipus, who will then marry his own mother, Jocasta. So, to avoid this drastic fate, Laius gave the baby Oedipus to a shepherd-servant to bring to a mountainside and be left to die there. But the shepherd took pity on the baby, passing him on to another shepherd who gave Oedipus to King Polybus and Queen Merope to raise as their own. When Oedipus grew up, he learned from the same Oracle at Delphi of the prophecy but, unaware of his true parentage, believed that he was destined to murder Polybus and marry Merope, so he left for Thebes to circumvent the fulfilment of the prophecy. On his way, he encountered an older man, killing him in a quarrel. Continuing on to Thebes, he found that the king of the city had been recently killed, and that the Thebans were at the mercy of a gigantic sphinx guarding entrance to the city. The menacing beast stopped Oedipus from entering, posing the riddle to him, discussed in the previous chapter. If Oedipus failed to give the correct answer, he would die instantly at the Sphinx's hands. But Oedipus came up with the answer.

As a result, the astonished Sphinx killed itself, allowing Oedipus to enter Thebes as a hero for having gotten rid of the terrible monster that had kept the city in captivity for so long. The Thebans asked Oedipus to be their king, to replace their previous king, Laius, who had been killed in a conflict. He accepted and married Jocasta, the widowed queen. Several years later, a plague struck Thebes. An oracle said it would end when King Laius's murderer had been driven from Thebes. Oedipus investigated the murder, discovering that Laius was the man he had killed on his way to Thebes. To his horror, he also learned that Laius was his real father and Jocasta his mother. In despair, Oedipus blinded himself and Jocasta hanged herself. Oedipus was then banished from Thebes. The prophecy pronounced at Delphi had come true.

The Oedipus legend provides one of the first narrative portraits of the notion of destiny (Rickman 2004). The constituent riddle in the narrative provides the key to understanding why destiny is inescapable—like the phases of a day, it is beyond human control. The exact same riddle is found broadly across ancient societies. suggesting that it is an unconscious archetype (Demish 1977; Clay 2003; Deekshitar 2004). In Philippine mythology, the sphinx is depicted as part human and part eagle; and it too asks the same kind of riddle to wanderers who trespass in the Bicol region. Anyone who fails to answer it carried off to the Mayon Volcano as an offering to the volcano god, Gev'ra, so as to appease his anger (Danesi 2020). The details vary from the Greek riddle, but its function and the metaphorical structure are the same (Taylor 1948, 1951; Köngas-Maranda 1976). As such, it leads to grasping the concept of destiny and mortality as unfolding in three phases: infancy, adulthood, and old age.

The belief in antiquity that riddles were somehow connected with destiny and mortality was a common one. It was believed, for example, that Homer's death was precipitated by the distress he felt at his failure to solve the following riddle posed to him by a group of fishermen:

> What we caught, we threw away. What we could not catch, we kept.
> (*Answer*: fleas or lice)

The Biblical story of Samson is another testament to this belief. At his wedding feast, Samson posed the following riddle to his Philistine guests, whom he mistrusted (Judges 14: 14):

> Out of the eater came forth meat and out of the strong came forth sweetness.
> (*Answer:* honey issuing from the carcass of a lion in which bees had constructed a beehive).

Samson gave the Philistines seven days to come up with the answer, convinced that they would be incapable of doing so. The deceitful guests took advantage of the time given to them to coerce the answer from Samson's paramour, Delilah. When they gave Samson the correct response, the mighty hero became enraged, declaring war against all Philistines. The ensuing conflict led eventually to his own destruction. All this came about over a riddle, which Samson had contrived to describe the fact that he had killed a young lion with his bare hands, noticing bees constructing a hive in the corpse after returning to it later—hence "sweetness" (honey) coming out of the lion's carcass.

As these historical examples also indicate, riddling is connected to wisdom and heroism. This is perhaps why the story is told about the Queen of Sheba, who traveled to Jerusalem to test the famed intellect and wisdom of King Solomon with riddles (Kings 10.1–3, Chronicles 9.1–12). The actual riddles are not found in the Biblical account of her visit but can be reconstructed retrospectively with the *Midrash Mishle* (Book of Proverbs), from the medieval period (from Lassner 1993, 162). Below is an example:

> How can a woman say to her son: "Your father is my father; your grandfather, my husband; you are my son, and I am your sister?"
> (*Solomon replied*: "The two daughters of Lot," who became pregnant by their father and bore sons).

The ancient and medieval riddles invariably revolved around understanding something intangible, or else how something relates to the human condition. An example of a common type is the *year* riddle, found across antiquity as a means to grasp the nature of time as it manifests itself in phases—extending the metaphor of the Sphinx's Riddle. The following one is from the *Greek Anthology* (chapter 1) (Paton 1927; Jay 1973):

> There is one father and twelve children; of these each has twice thirty daughters of different appearance. Some are white to look at and the others black in turn. They are immortal and yet they all fade away.
> (*Answer:* the year and its component parts or phases: father = year, twelve children = twelve months, daughters = night and day, immortal = the year is always the same, fading = the parts (days, months) come and go)

This is similar to the Sanskrit riddle discussed in the previous chapter—the difference being that the mapping involved the image of a wheel in the former, in contrast to the image of a family source domain in the present case, whereby the members of a family are mapped onto the "members" (parts) of the year, thus connecting them ontologically. Such riddles reveal a generic linkage of *time* and *life*. Another example of this connection from the *Greek Anthology* is the following one:

> My mother I bring forth, she brings forth me. I'm sometimes greater, sometimes less than she.
> (*Answer*: night and day)

In addition to providing understanding of metaphysical concepts, the early riddles also had a situation-specific phenomenological function, casting light on the nature of certain things, rather than providing a metaphysical image schema. This type of function became particularly prominent in the early medieval period. Below are examples from the *Greek Anthology*:

> I look at you whene'er you look at me. You see but I see not; no sight have I.
> (*Answer*: a mirror. The riddle personifies the mirror so as to bring out its primary function or characteristic—reflection ("I look at you"), which allows someone to "see" oneself, even though the mirror itself has no vision)

> A wingless bird, fleeting to heaven from earth. Each eye that meets me weeps, but not from grief. And in thin air I vanish at my birth.
> (*Answer:* smoke. The riddle portrays smoke in terms of its physical features, namely that it: (a) exists as a suspension in the air, and hence its similarity to a "wingless bird," and (b) that it quickly dissipates ("in thin air I vanish at my birth"). It also highlights an effect it will have on humans—"Each eye that meets me weeps")

> A blackened lump am I, and fire begat me.
> (*Answer*: pitch. This riddle animates pitch, whereby it describes itself as a "blackened lump" and how it originates—"fire begat me")

As the examples above illustrate, the two functions of the early riddles—metaphysical and phenomenological—were designed to engender understanding of things, abstract or physical. The following table presents a sampling of the phenomenological function in Norse mythology—the legend of King Heidrek (Henrikson 1998).

As Archer Taylor (1951, 3) points out, discussing the functional and image schematic similarity of such riddles in hundreds of ancient-medieval cultures (Chinese, Hungarian, Russian, Philippine, Finnish, and others), the presence of the same pattern of source domains suggests that riddling is an "art of understanding," realized by both metaphysical and phenomenological

**Table 2.1 Phenomenological Riddles**

| Riddle | Understanding | Source Domain(s) |
|---|---|---|
| Four hang, four sprang, two point the way, two to ward off dogs, one dangles after, always rather dirty. (*Answer:* a cow) | The cow's mammary glands and how they are oriented, two of which are used for self-defense | *Image schema:* dangling |
| Mankind it mars, speech it hinders, yet speech it will inspire. (*Answer:* alcoholic drink) | Alcohol's effects on speech, both slurring and stimulating it | *Image schemas:* (a) the obstacle schema ("hinders"), (b) the impairment schema ("mars"), and (c) inhalation ("inspire") |
| From home, I went. From home, I made my way. I saw a road of roads, and a road under them, and a road over them, and a road on all sides. What are we? (*Answer:* rivers) | The structure and movement of rivers; the riddle is formulated in terms of a personification of a natural object, portraying what rivers allow people to do, that is, travel | *Image schemas:* (a) habitation (river source); (b) path ("road") |
| What is that whines on high, the armlathe howls, and they're hard? (*Answer:* arrows) | The sounds made by arrows and their rigidity | *Image schemas:* animal sounds (whining, howling) |

metaphorical mappings. The former are archetypal and the latter situation specific.

## DELECTATION

As mentioned in the previous chapter, riddling developed ludic functions in early societies, as these moved away from their mythic origins. They are among the first archeological artifacts documenting the use of language for delectation and entertainment, thus providing indirect evidence of how language started subserving social discourse functions. Riddles became part of many ancient feasts, such as the Greek symposia or the Roman Saturnalia, as intrinsic components of the recreational rituals. Many of these became part of storytelling featuring the riddle contests as their theme. Known as *riddle-tales*, they are examples of the move away from mythic to a more descriptive narrativity. Starting in the early medieval period, riddles also developed a literary-aesthetic function in tandem with the ludic one, as discussed in chapter 1, appearing in many collections that were seemingly used at feasts or gatherings. The language of those riddles is typically stylized poetry. At the same time, riddles were perceived to have pedagogical value—raising awareness in people (especially children) of the ambiguities of discourse. In due course, riddles started appearing in narratives aimed primarily at children, such as the fairy tales of the Brothers Grimm and the Mother Goose nursery rhymes.

As discussed, this evolution of riddles—*mythic-ludic-literary-pedagogical*—mirrors the evolution of language from a poetic stage based in *mythos* to subsequent stages based in *lógos*. It can even be suggested that the sense of delectation itself emerged as a result of the riddle contests and riddle-tales, constituting a means to play with language and gain enjoyment from it. As Potamiti (2015, 134) aptly observes, "The ludic dimension of folklore is perhaps better manifested in no other verbal folklore genre than in riddles, also a play genre."

One of the first collections documenting the rise of the ludic function is the *Greek Anthology* (mentioned above), which has been dated as early as the seventh century BCE and as late as 1000 CE (Jay 1973). There are sixteen books in the anthology; the riddles are found in book 13. All indications are that the riddles were meant to entertain people and were likely orated by anyone who could read at gatherings such as dinners and feasts. Some the riddles are truly challenging, requiring rather sophisticated knowledge of Greek mythology and history (Hovanec 1978, 15):

> If you put one hundred in the middle of a burning fire, you will find the son and a slayer of a virgin
> (*Answer*: Pyrrhus).

This is actually an early blend of an enigma and a charade (discussed below), since it is solved by putting the Greek symbol for 100, *rho*, into the word *pyros*, "fire," producing the name *Pyrrhos (Pyrrhus)*, who was the son of Deidamia and the slayer of Polyxena. Solving this riddle requires specific knowledge, since it refers to the spelling of the word required within the statement. Ludic riddles were designed to be challenging, as they often provided humorous social critique, such as castigating a dreadful host at a party, making fun of someone's nose, memorializing a dead hero satirically, and the like, which can be seen in many riddle collections, from the *Greek Anthology* to the *Aenigmata Symphosii*. In the latter work, Symphosius asserts explicitly in the preface that he composed them to be used at the festivities during the Roman Saturnalia (Sebo 2009). In his *Symposium*, Plato (1951) gave a similar account of how riddles were central to the success of a *symposium* (banquet). As Naerebout and Beerden 2013, 140) write,

> In the competitive Greek societies, words were a primary locus of competition: there can be no doubt about the popularity of wordplay in the Greek world. Riddles shared in this popularity: sympotic riddles are particularly well attested—it seems there was no symposium without a fair number of riddles. The contest-riddle was a known form of riddling. So riddling pervaded Greek life on many levels and during many occasions.

Competitive riddle games are found across the world (Taylor 1951). The Hindu epic, *Mahabharata* (c. 400 CE), describes riddle contests not unlike those of ancient Greece and Rome (Kaivola-Bregenhøj 2017). These are situation specific, reflecting cultural emphases, typically describing common objects, people, and events in metaphorical ways (Cook 2009), as the following riddles from *Aenigmata Symposii* illustrate (Hickman 1912). Note that personification or animation of objects is the core strategy, thus imbuing them with human qualities anthropomorphically, whereby image schemas referring to humans form the basis for inferring the properties of nonhuman entities in order to make efficient descriptions or judgments about them. Research has shown that this is a universal property of mentation, appearing early in childhood understanding (Symphosius, *The Hundred Riddles of Symphosius*, Internet Archive, https://archive.org/stream/hundredriddless00sympgoog/hundredriddless00sympgoog_djvu.txt):

> *A Mule*
> Unlike my mother, in semblance different; from my father, of mingled race, a breed; unfit for progeny, of others am I born, and; none is born of me.
> [*Explanation:* This riddle is allusive—referring to the mule as the offspring of a donkey and a horse (animals of "mingled race" and "of others am I born") and sterile ("none is born of me").]
>
> *A Reed* (an early writing instrument)
> Sweet darling of the banks, always close to the depths, sweetly I sing for the Muses; when drenched with black, I am the tongue's messenger by guiding fingers pressed.
> [*Explanation:* Reeds for writing grow in water ("sweet darling of the banks"), and writing was used at first mainly for poetry ("I sing for the Muses") and executed with black ink ("drenched with black"). As a substitution of oral speech ("the tongue's messenger"), the riddle asserts that writing is carried out by "guiding fingers pressed." The analogy of a writing instrument as the "tongue's

messenger" is truly ingenious, since it indicates awareness of the relation of writing to speech.]

*An Echo*
A modest maid, too well I observe the law of modesty; I am not pert in speech nor rash of tongue; of my own accord I will not speak, but I answer him who speaks.
[*Explanation:* An echo "will not speak," but will "answer him who speaks," since it involves a physical reflection of vocal words. By itself, therefore, it cannot be "pert in speech" or "rash of tongue," alluding to the expectation that speech be "modest."]

*A Key*
Great powers from little strength I bring. I open closed houses, but again I close the open. I guard the house for the master, but in turn am guarded by him.
[*Explanation:* This describes what keys do ("open closed houses") and guard a house for its master (by keeping it locked). The master will guard the key itself, because it has "great powers" to do the guarding with "little strength."]

*A Hammer*
I do not lay claim to strength for my body as a whole, but in a battle of heads I refuse to strive with none; large is my head, my whole weight too therein.
[*Explanation:* The anthropomorphic image schemas underlying this riddle relate to the hammer's "body" = its handle and its large "head," which can strike someone forcefully in a "battle of heads."]

*A Frog*
I give vent to hoarse sounds in the water's midst, but my voice with praise resounds, as if it too were sounding its own praises; and though I am ever singing, no one praises my songs.
[*Explanation:* A frog's "hoarse sounds" are its croaks, which it bellows from "the water's midst" (a pond); but these are hardly melodious sounds, that is, "songs," and thus nobody will ever "praise them."]

Similar riddles are documented across ancient and medieval societies (Taylor 1948). A riddle with the same kind of fascination with writing as the one above, and with the same allusive structure, is found in a ninth century Italian manuscript. It is the first written document to show a conscious use of a *volgare* (a language of the people), rather than Latin; it is a four-line riddle written in an early form of the Veronese dialect, and hence called the *Indovinello veronese* (Migliorini 1987). The manuscript is preserved in Verona in the Biblioteca Capitolare. The traditional interpretation of the riddle is that the author is writing with a pen that is "prodding his oxen to plow white fields" (that is, writing on white paper) as it is "sowing black seed" (ink):

> He prodded his oxen to move forward
> plowing white fields
> and a white plow he held
> sowing black seed.

Some questions regarding the language of the *Indovinello* have been debated in the relevant literature. However, the interpretation above is supported by the fact that the meaning of *parare* as "to prod oxen to move forward" continues in the contemporary dialect of Verona and fits in with the overall meaning of the riddle, in which "white fields," "plow," and "black seed" represent aspects of writing metaphorically. Riddles were among the first forms to be written down and are thus valuable philological documents for examining the evolution of writing functions over time.

A scholar who wrote riddles for pure delectation and for engaging one's interlocutor cleverly was Alcuin (chapter 1). He sent the following one to the Archbishop of Mainz, known by the nickname of Damoeta, to express gratitude after receiving a gift from him (Alcuin, *Lectures Delivered in the Cathedral Church of Bristol,* Internet Archive, https://archive.org/stream/alcuinofyorklect00brow/alcuinofyorklect00brow_djvu.txt):

> A beast has sudden come to this my house,
> A beast of wonder, who two heads has got,
> And yet the beast has only one jaw-bone.
> Twice three times ten of horrid teeth it has.
> Its food grows on this body of mine,
> Not flesh, nor fruit. It eats not with its teeth,
> Drinks not. Its open mouth shows no decay.
> Tell me, Damoeta dear, what beast is this?
> (*Answer*: a comb)

The solution hinges on decoding the metaphorical meaning of *beast* as a device (a comb) rather than an animal, which likely was a source of delectation for its intended reader. Via this anthropomorphic source domain, the elements of a comb can then be linked to human and animal anatomy and behaviors: combs with *two heads* were common in the era, possessing tines (prongs) on two sides, installed on one *jaw-bone* (comb shaft), which holds the *teeth*. The comb's *food* is head hair, which *grows on this body of mine.* Alcuin expected a reply ("Tell me, Damoeta dear, what beast is this?"), indicating that riddling was becoming a kind of clever communicative discourse. As Sorrell (1996, 311) aptly points out, this particular riddle constituted a perfect example of what situation-specific riddling was all about—a means of shedding light and critiquing everyday life, including its trivial objects:

> The presentation of a *de luxe* comb of elephant ivory by Archbishop Riculf of Mainz to his friend Alcuin of York in c. 794 provided the occasion for two replies, one in a prose letter and the other in a verse epistle, in which Riculf's gift is playfully transformed into the subject of a descriptive riddle. This . . . shows the Anglo-Saxon riddle mentality at work in the transformation of an artifact into an animate being, whereby the various elements of the comb are described in terms of the head and mouthparts of a formidable creature.

Most of Alcuin's riddles are found in his *Disputatio regalis et nobilissimi juvenis Pippini cum Albino scholastico* ("Dialogue of Pepin, the Most Noble and Royal Youth, with the Teacher Albinus"), a document written in the form of riddle dialogues in which he himself, Alcuin (also called Albinus), converses with a twelve-year-old Pippin, the second son of Charlemagne, and one of his own pupils (Sorrell 1996). Below is an example:

> What is it that makes bitter things sweet?
> (*Answer:* hunger).
>
> This riddle works via implication—namely, when someone experiences hunger, then even food that may taste bitter will taste sweet.

The riddles of Aldhelm (chapter 1) also have a similar communicative, situation-specific function. He included them in a treatise he wrote for the King of Northumbria, becoming one of the most widely quoted texts of the medieval period, in large part because of the riddles, which were, again, about everyday things (animals, plants, household items, and so on) and their social meanings. Two examples are the following (Aldhelm, *The Riddles of Aldhelm,* https://archive.org/details/riddlesofaldhelm0000aldh):

> Long since, the holy power that made all things
> So made me that my master's dangerous foes
> I scatter. Bearing weapons in my jaws,
> I soon decide fierce combats; yet I flee
> Before the lashings of a little child.
> (*Answer*: a dog companion)
>
> I share with the surf one destiny
> In rolling cycles when each month repeats.
> As beauty in my brilliant form retreats,

So too the surges fade in cresting sea.
(*Answer*: the moon)

Both riddles cast metaphorical light on each topic: for example, *weapons* = dog's teeth, *brilliant form* = lunar light. Like those of Symphosius, Aldhelm's riddles deal with the specific world of the medieval era, constituting an indirect historiography of the era via the riddle-based interpretation of its objects and events—that is, the meanings of natural phenomena such as the wind or the moon, of animals such as dogs, and the like are presented through the riddle format, allowing us to imagine life and things in the era through this format.

## AESTHETICS

As mentioned in the previous chapter, riddle anthologies were designed in a literary-aesthetic fashion early on. One such collection is the anonymous *Exeter Book* (c. 960), which contains nearly a hundred riddles, composed as miniature riddle-poems about everyday things such as storms, ships, beer, books, and falcons (Gameson 1996). The book thus constitutes a portrait of medieval English life with its inherent values and anxieties, such as the meaning of suffering and the passage of time (Chambers, Förster, and Flower 1933). The same type of poetic style for characterizing everyday life surfaces in riddle traditions across cultures. For example, the collection by the Persian Amir Khusro (1253–1325), written in the Indic language Hindawi, contains 286 riddles divided into six themes that covered concepts similar to those in the *Exeter Book* (Vatuk 1969). Below is an example from the latter book (*The Exeter Book*, Internet Archive, https://archive.org/details/exeterbook0000unse):

> Through the mouth speaking many voices,
> I sing in modulations. I frequently exchange
> kindred voices—I cry out aloud—I keep my counsel.
> I do not conceal my voice.
>
> I bring back the minstrel of bygone evenings to earls—
> and bliss to cities when I cry aloud
> in the voice of its citizens. Unmoving they sit listening in their homes.
> Say what I am called, who
> so clearly imitates a feasting song—
> who loudly proclaims to men
> many welcome things by my voice.

(*Answer:* a nightingale)

As can be seen, the nightingale is described in terms of the kind of enjoyable things it brings to human ears—*modulations, the minstrel of bygone evenings, welcome things*, and the like. After the advent of typesetting in the middle part of the 1400s, making print materials abundant and inexpensive, collections of riddles were among the first books printed, indicating that reading for pleasure was one of the first offshoots of the spread of literacy. By the late Renaissance, riddles were being tailored more and more to produce humorous or whimsical literary effects, reflecting an increasingly secular leisure culture interested in literary delectation. One of the first book of riddles intended purely for recreational reading, called *Demaundes Joyous* ("Amusing Questions"), was published in England in 1511 by a printer called Wynkyn de Worde (a suggestive eponymic name), which includes the famous paradoxical conundrum: *Which came first, the hen or the egg?* Here are several riddles from the book, illustrating the style which may be a source of subsequent one-line jokes:

How many calves' tails would it take to reach from the earth to the sky? (*Answer*: No more than one, if it be long enough.)

Why do men make an oven in a town?
(*Answer:* Because they cannot make a town in an oven.)

How may a man discern a cow in a flock of sheep?
(*Answer:* By his eyesight.)

Why does a cow lie down?
(*Answer:* Because it cannot sit.)

What is it that never freezes?
(*Answer:* Boiling water.)

Another well-known English riddle collection of the era, *The Merry Book of Riddles*, utilized a humorous stye as well, but with a more elaborate poetic language (Schiltz 2015). Below is an example from that work, which found its way into later collections (from *Humour, Wit, & Satire,* Internet Archive, https://archive.org/stream/gri_33125015242841/gri_33125015242841_djvu.txt):

He went to the wood and caught it,
He sate him downe and sought it;
Because he could not finde it,

Home with him he brought it.
(*Answer*: a thorn caught on a foot or alternatively lice)

What stands out is the riddle's cleverness, combining wordplay with a situation-specific image schematic source domain aiming to deceive the reader, drawing attention away from the answer with allusive-ambiguous verbs (*caught, sought, could not finde*), which could refer to virtually anything present in the *wood*.

As literacy spread, riddling attracted all kinds of intellectuals, scientists, and philosophers. Among them was Leonardo da Vinci, who wrote a set of "prophecies" in the form of riddles, in which he portrayed hypothetical scenarios that the reader was challenged to figure out (providing his own answers to each one). The prophecies were written on sheets in the *Codex Atlanticus* (1478–1519), a collection of da Vinci's writings and drawings compiled after his death by the Milanese sculptor Pompeo Leoni and now preserved in the Biblioteca Ambrosiana in Milan. The prophecies seem, on the surface, to predict things to come, but the answers quickly dispel this supposition with their reference to everyday things and notions:

Men will be borne up on the feathers of flying creatures.
(*Answer:* feather beds)

Many will have their little ones taken from them and slaughtered and cruelly quartered.
(*Answer:* sheep, cows, and goats)

Many will make homes for themselves in entrails and live in their own entrails.
(*Answer:* sausages which are put into entrails)

These convey a wry sense of humor, probably designed to ridicule the practice of prophecy that was in vogue at the time, deriding it as anachronistic in an age of scientific humanism—if vague enough, any prediction can be thought to come true. The growth in popularity of riddle collections, such as the one by da Vinci, for seemingly trivial reasons, was met by acerbic critiques. The Italian writer Baldassare Castiglione attacked them in his *Libro del cortegiano* (1528) as instigations at promoting insincerity among people, and thus as going against the ideals of virtue that humanism wanted to espouse.

It was in the eighteenth century that riddles became highly popular literary artifacts, included as regular features in newspapers and periodicals (Taylor 1951; Abrahams 1972). Writers, poets, and philosophers constructed them to probe the nature of things metaphorically. Voltaire, for instance, would often compose ingenious riddles, such as the following one, simply for the sake of it (from Voltaire, *The Project Gutenberg eBook of Voltaire's Romances*, Project Gutenberg, https://www.gutenberg.org/files/35595/35595.txt):

> What of all things in the world is the longest, the shortest, the swiftest, the slowest, the most divisible and most extended, most regretted, most neglected, without which nothing can be done, and with which many do nothing, which destroys all that is little and ennobles all that is great?
> (*Answer*: time)

Describing time as *long, swift, slow, divisible, extended*, and so on is so common in everyday discourse that we are hardly aware that these expressions are part of a conceptual metaphorical formula that envisions *time* as a *physical entity*. So popular had riddling become, that the subsequent nineteenth century saw the crystallization of three literary riddle genres—the charade, the enigma, and the conundrum (chapter 1). To reiterate here, the *charade* is solved by unraveling the meanings of the separate syllables, words, or lines in its statement. Consider the following nineteenth-century charade, contained in *The Boy's Own Book*, published in London in 1828:

> My first is to ramble;
> My next to retreat;
> My whole oft enrages
> In summer's fierce heat.
> Who Am I?
> (*Answer*: a gadfly)

The first line plays on the meaning of the word *gad* as "to move about restlessly," and the second on the dual meanings of the verb *fly*: "to flee or retreat from something" and "a dipterous insect." The subsequent two lines complete the description of the gadfly as an irritating insect. In charades, typically, the phrase *my first* refers to the first syllable of a word, *my second* to the second syllable, and *my whole* to the entire word. The charade is the source of the corresponding game that originated in the nineteenth century called the *mime charade*, played by members of separate teams who act out the various syllables of a word, an entire word, or a phrase in pantomime.

The charade spread as a literary genre, adopted by various famous writers. The following one by Lewis Carroll, which he included in his *Phantasmagoria, and Other Poems* (1869), is a case in point:

> My First is singular at best:
> More plural is my Second:

My Third is far the pluralest—
So plural-plural, I protest
It scarcely can be reckoned!

My First is followed by a bird:
My Second by believers
In magic art: my simple Third
Follows, too often, hopes absurd
And plausible deceivers.

My First to get at wisdom tries—
A failure melancholy!
My Second men revered as wise:
My Third from heights of wisdom flies
To depths of frantic folly.

My First is ageing day by day:
My Second's age is ended:
My Third enjoys an age, they say,
That never seems to fade away,
Through centuries extended.

My Whole? I need a poet's pen
To paint her myriad phases:
The monarch, and the slave, of men—
A mountain-summit, and a den
Of dark and deadly mazes—

A flashing light—a fleeting shade—
Beginning, end, and middle
Of all that human art hath made
Or wit devised! Go, seek her aid,
If you would read my riddle!
(*Answer:* imagination)

As Carroll subsequently explained (Carroll 1883), the solution is what the entire riddle is about, the *imagination*—a faculty of mind that *scarcely can be reckoned* and is best described by *a poet's pen*. The answer has three syllables indicated in the riddle as follows:

*My First is singular at best* = first person singular subject pronoun, *I*.
*My second men revered as wise* = *magi(cians)* were once considered wise wizards.
*My Third enjoys an age* = *nation*

*Imagination* = I + magi + nation

Another well-known literary charade of the same era was composed by English writer Jane Austen, which she included in her 1816 novel, *Emma*:

> When my first is a task to a young girl of spirit,
> And my second confines her to finish the piece,
> How hard is her fate! but how great is her merit,
> If by taking my whole she effects her release!
> (*Answer*: hemlock)

The breakdown is as follows:

> *My first is a task to a young girl of spirit* = in Austen's era, "a young girl of spirit," would be expected to sew and thus would know how to make *hem*. *My second confines her to finish the piece* = *lock* is a synonym for *confine*.
> The final two lines are a plea for women to liberate themselves from the banal social plight in which they find themselves.

An enigma (chapter 1) is a rhyming riddle that contains one or more veiled references to the answer. The following well-known one was composed by the British statesman George Canning and is included in many collections (from *Spelling Books,* Internet Archive, https://archive.org/stream/spellingforgrades _202002/simplificationof00harl_djvu.txt):

> A word there is of plural number,
> Foe to ease and tranquil slumber;
> Any other word you take
> And add an "s" will plural make,
> But if you add an "s" to this,
> So strange the metamorphosis;
> Plural is plural now no more,
> And sweet what bitter was before.
> (*Answer*: cares - caress)

The word *cares* is *foe to ease and tranquil slumber* and is of *plural number*. By adding an "s" to this word—*caress*—the result is a word that is *plural no more*, which turns the meaning of *cares* on its head by making *sweet what bitter was before*.

The English politician and writer, Horace Walpole, came up with the following ingenious enigma, which is based on how we use specific adverbs in relating the days of the week to each other in temporal terms (from *British*

*Word Puzzles*, Digital Commons, https://digitalcommons.butler.edu/cgi/viewcontent.cgi?article=1737&context=wordways):

> Before my birth I had a name,
> But soon as born I chang'd the same;
> And when I'm laid within the tomb,
> I shall my father's name assume.
> I change my name three days together
> Yet live but one in any weather.
> (*Answer*: today)

Before its "birth," *today* has a different name—*tomorrow*. For example, if *today* is Monday, then from the perspective of the day before, Sunday, it is labeled *tomorrow*. And when it is *laid within the tomb*, that is, when it is over, it takes a new name—*yesterday*: that is, when Tuesday comes about, Monday is over, and we refer to it as *yesterday*. Finally, though it lasts only one day, it changes its name three days in a row (*three days together*): from yesterday, to today, to tomorrow.

The conundrum is a riddle that plays on words, such as the use of homophony, as this following conundrum shows (Barrick 1974):

> What is black and white and red all over?
> (*Answer*: a newspaper)

The words *red* and *read* are homophones, although they are spelled differently. This riddle has appeared in many American publications since at least 1917, constituting what some riddle scholars call a *folk riddle*—a riddle that becomes part of an unconscious folk culture. As Delia Chiaro (1992) observes, such riddles are virtually impossible to translate into other languages, because they play on the specific meanings, structures, and forms of a particular language, not on any abstract metaphysical notion.

In the nineteenth century a movement emerged that intentionally utilized riddling for ironic-satirical effect, called the *literary nonsense* movement. The origin of the movement can likely be traced to the popularity of the nursery rhymes of Mother Goose—a pseudonym found in Charles Perrault's collection of fairy tales, *Les contes de ma mere l'Oye*, translated in English as *Tales of My Mother Goose* (1697). An example of a nonsense riddle from this collection is the following one:

> Hey, diddle, diddle,
> The cat and the fiddle,
> The cow jumped over the moon;
> The little dog laughed

To see such sport,
And the dish ran away with the spoon.

This is designed to resist any specific answer or interpretation. Searching for a meaning is itself nonsensical—inducing a kind of circular reasoning that never comes to a conceptual point. Lewis Carroll became fascinated by the nonsense trend in literature. As Victoria Kennedy (2019) has astutely commented, Carroll's children's novels and poetry, especially *Alice's Adventures in Wonderland* (1865), have a strong appeal in large part because of "the unique literary nonsense aspects of *Alice*," which "demonstrate its enduring intellectual integrity." As she goes on to illustrate, one of the first examples of Carroll's nonsense style can be seen in the following riddle posed at the Mad Hatter's tea party in the novel:

"Why is a raven like a writing desk?"
 "No. I give up," Alice replied. "What's the answer?"
 "I haven't the slightest idea," said the Hatter.
 Alice sighed wearily. "I think you might do something better with time than wasting it in asking silly riddles."
 "If you knew Time like I know time you wouldn't talk about wasting it. Time is not an 'it.' It's a 'him.' So there!"

Readers were so frustrated by the lack of an answer in the novel that Carroll was compelled to provide one subsequently—*nevar*—which, as Francis Huxley (1976) writes, was not an answer at all:

Because it can produce a few notes, though they are very flat; and is *nevar* put with the wrong end in the front! [Carroll's answer.] This, however, is merely an afterthought: the riddle, as originally invented, had no answer at all.

Carroll's answer of *nevar* seems at first to be a misspelling of *never*. But in typical Carrollian style, it is the word *raven* spelled backward, which still is not an answer to the Mad Hatter's riddle. One of Carroll's most salient examples of nonsense writing is his poem about the killing of a strange creature called the Jabberwock, which he included in *Through the Looking-Glass, and What Alice Found There* (1871). In the poem many of the words are nonsensical, constituting riddles in their own right as to what they might mean. They appear to be legitimate English words, constructed with the normal grammatical and phonetic structure of words in that language, but they have no ascribed meaning. Carroll had, in effect, disconnected form from meaning, leaving it up to the imagination of the reader to figure out what they could possibly mean.

The poem is presented in an early scene in which Alice encounters the White King and the White Queen, whereupon she finds a book written in an unintelligible language. Realizing that she is in the inverted world of the magical Looking-Glass House, she recognizes that the verses on the pages are written in mirror-writing. So, she holds a mirror to the poem and reads the reflected verse of *Jabberwocky*. The first stanza is given below:

> 'Twas brillig, and the slithy toves
> Did gyre and gimble in the wabe;
> All mimsy were the borogoves,
> And the mome raths outgrabe.

When Alice finished reading the poem, she gives her impressions as follows:

"It seems very pretty," she said when she had finished it, "but it's rather hard to understand!" (You see she didn't like to confess, even to herself, that she couldn't make it out at all.) "Somehow it seems to fill my head with ideas— only I don't exactly know what they are! However, somebody killed something: that's clear, at any rate."

Jabberwocky words have no conventional meaning, just suggestive meaning, that comes from blending words or parts of words together to form new words, as for example:

- *Jabberwock*: Carroll himself stated that it is a blend of the Anglo-Saxon word *wocor* meaning "offspring" with *jabber* in its ordinary meaning of "excited and voluble discussion" (Tenniel 2003, 328–331).
- *Brillig*: A meaning is given to this word in another part of the novel, when Humpty Dumpty comments, "Brillig means four o'clock in the afternoon, the time when you begin broiling things for dinner."
- *Wabe*: Alice suggests that this might mean "the grass-plot around a sundial," to which Humpty Dumpty retorts, "Of course, it is," because it "goes a long way before it, and a long way behind it." Carroll himself later stated that a *wabe* is "the side of a hill (from its being soaked by rain)" (Tenniel 2003, 331).

So influential was this poem in English literature that some Jabberwocky words subsequently entered the English lexicon, including *chortle* ("laugh in a gleeful way")*, galumph* ("move in a clumsy manner"), and *jabberwocky* itself as a synonym for nonsense. Carroll was fascinated by the boundless range of meanings that language has the potential to encode. By inventing new words, he likely also wanted to show his readers that a language leaves many conceptual gaps. Words such as *brillig, slithy, tove,* and *wabe* are all concepts for which no specific English words existed, filling in the existential void that may have existed. Their meanings work via association—by inference with existing words, a feature of metaphor itself (chapter 4). And indeed if English-speaking people started using the Jabberwocky words routinely, then after a while they would start "seeing" or "recognizing" *brilligs, slithy things, toves,* and *wabes* everywhere, eventually believing that the things they refer to must exist.

The nonsense movement did not emerge in a historical vacuum. As discussed, riddles were part of ludic traditions even in antiquity, devised to entertain and, often, to bring out the inanity of human actions and ideas. Oral folk traditions are replete with such riddles. A writer who became a champion of nonsense literature was English humorist Edward Lear, whose two books, *A Book of Nonsense* (1845) and *Laughable Lyrics* (1877), popularized limericks. Below is an example:

> There was an Old Man with a beard,
> Who said, "It is just as I feared!—
> Two Owls and a Hen,
> Four Larks and a Wren,
> Have all built their nests in my beard!"

Such limericks could easily be turned into riddles by simply eliminating their first lines (which constitute answers). As the literary nonsense movement emphasized, the ludic function of language, which started with the ancient riddles, riddle games, and riddle-tales, shows how discourse functions often emerge not from strictly communicative needs but also from what can be called an "aesthetics of sense," that is, an enjoyment of the ways in which riddling casts light on things in its own unique ways. In a relevant work, Cornelius Gulere (2012) similarly argues that we hardly ever realize that riddling occurs in everyday discourses, given its appeal, imparting a sense of clever understanding that is likely embedded in the metaphorical structures of discursive interactions.

## PEDAGOGY

The spread of riddle books in the 1500s designed explicitly for imparting literacy in an enjoyable way highlighted the ever-broadening pedagogical functions of riddling (Launaud 2009). As Anthony Mollica (2019) has observed, this aspect of riddles is particularly important in imparting aesthetically or humorously how language and unexpected thoughts can be so cleverly intertwined. As discussed above, the riddles of Wynkyn de Worde in England were one-line riddle jokes that had pedagogical resonance; similarly in Italy the riddles of Bertoldo, a character created by Giulio Cesare Croce in the sixteenth century, became a staple of schooling in Italy until recently. They too are one-liners uttered by Bertoldo, a cunning peasant who lived at the time of the Veronese court of Alboino, the Lombard king. The riddles entertained common folk because they made fun of popes, nobility, and rustic people alike. One of the best-known examples is the following one:

> What is the best wine?
> (*Answer:* The one you drink at other people's homes)

Riddles can actually be classified in terms of their potential pedagogical uses or applications.

- *Enigmas*: These are designed to induce a conscious focus on specific aspects of language itself: *What always comes at the start of November?* (*Answer:* The letter "*N*" which always starts the word "*November*"). The phraseology of the riddle is intended to dupe us into deciphering the phrase "*the start of November*" as a time period rather than as a reference to the spelling of the word *November.* Here is another example: *What has four eyes but cannot see?* (*Answer:* Mississippi). The letter "*i*" and the word *eye* are pronounced in the same way.
- *Charades*: These also can be used pedagogically to engender a sense of the relation between word structure and meaning, especially in compound words: *My first is a limb, my second is a round object; together they make an oval thing* (*Answer*: football).
- *Phenomenological riddles*: *It is round and goes round and round, never stopping. What is it?* (*Answer:* The Earth). The riddle's use of the image schema of orbital movement is potentially open-ended, but the phrase, *never stopping*, is suggestive of the orbital movement of planets, thus constraining the response. Another example is *It dwells deep and speaks all the languages of the world. What is it?* (*Answer:* an echo). The phrase *speaks all languages of the world* leads one to think of some person or entity that somehow can speak all languages. The expression *dwells deep*, however, is the key for unraveling the actual answer.
- *Conundrums*: *What can be either theatrical or sporty?* (*Answer:* play)—the word *play* refers to both a theatrical representation or to the act of executing a sport (as in *to play soccer*). Such riddles are useful for highlighting the presence of ambiguity and double entendre in language.

Perhaps the term that can be enlisted opportunely to explain why riddles may be effective pedagogically is *lateral thinking*—a term first used by Maltese physician and psychologist Edward De Bono (1970). It applies perfectly to how riddles are solved, since the answer is unexpected or surprising—that is, riddles impel us to break away from thinking literally as a default form of understanding. As Robert Sternberg (1985) has argued, riddles, like any puzzle, involve the activation of associative mechanisms, for fleshing out the nonobvious relationship between the information in the puzzle and the allusive, different meanings it might entail. Moreover, riddles can be used to portray the same concept in differential ways—hence their highly versatile pedagogical utility (Bar-Hillel, Noah, and Frederick 2018). For example, in his book *Children's Riddling*, John McDowell (1979, 135–146) shows how *locomotion* can be portrayed through riddles in terms of its different enablers or carriers:

>What has eight wheels and rolls?
>(*Answer:* roller skates)
>
>What has two wheels and pedals?
>(*Answer:* a bicycle)
>
>What has four wheels, no pedals, and a steering wheel?
>(*Answer:* a car)
>
>What has four legs and can run?
>(*Answer:* a mustang)
>
>What has three wheels and pedals?
>(*Answer:* a tricycle)
>
>What has four legs and can't walk?
>(*Answer:* a chair)
>
>What has long legs and it's hard to walk?
>(*Answer:* a seagull)

These features of riddles make it obvious why they have had pedagogical functions since the early civilizations. As Archer Taylor (1948, 3) has remarked, the historical record shows, in fact, that "the oldest recorded riddles are Babylonian school texts, from oral tradition that a teacher has put into a schoolbook." Their main learning focus is the activation of the awareness of the connection between language and thought.

## EPILOGUE

Riddles emerge in tandem with the foundational myths of a culture—they are either embedded within them (as the Riddle of the Sphinx) or else formulated separately. The conceptual metaphors inherent in them are traces to how language itself originated to subserve metaphysical understanding, on the basis of universal image schemas—*journeys, phases, wheels, cycles*, and so on. The power of metaphor to engender understanding may be the reason why riddling was perceived to be the language of oracles. It is also the founding conceptual strategy behind rituals, symbols, and other cultural artifacts (chapter 5). Often it is difficult to differentiate between connective metaphorical reasoning in antiquity from a metonymic (part-whole) reasoning. As an example, consider the *face is the person* conceptual formula, which has both a mapping structure (*face* onto *person*) and a metonymic structure (a part of the body, the *face*, to stand for the entire *person*). Whatever the conceptual basis of this concept, it is the reason why masks are used in many types of rituals, as symbols of personality. In ancient Greece, the word *persona* signified a "mask" worn by an actor on stage. Subsequently, it came to have the meaning of "the personality of the stage character," after masks were no longer used. This meaning can still be seen in the theater term *dramatis personae* "cast of characters" (literally "the persons of the drama"). Eventually, the word came to have its present meaning of "living human being." This explains why we continue to use theatrical metaphors such as *to play a role in life, to put on a proper face*, and so forth in reference to persons.

Starting with the earliest mythic riddles, and then with the ludic, literary, and pedagogical riddles, the overall purpose of riddling seems to be understanding the world, creating associations, filling in gaps, casting light on the things of everyday life, and so on. The mythic riddles are the ones that are of direct relevance here—and hence will be the subject matter of the remainder of this book. The understanding that they imply is a root (primary) form. From the conceptual metaphors that they embed comes all subsequent understanding.

In 1922, Ludwig Wittgenstein became fascinated by how language presented information about the world, via simple imagistic propositions about world facts. He developed what came to be called a picture theory of language by which propositions represent features of the world in the same way that pictures do. Wittgenstein subsequently had serious misgivings about his theory of language. In his posthumously published *Philosophical Investigations* (1953), he was perplexed by the fact that language could do much more than just construct propositions about the world. So, he introduced the idea of "language games," by which he claimed that there existed a variety of linguistic games (describing, reporting, guessing riddles, making jokes, and so on) that went beyond simple information processing. Wittgenstein had obviously become convinced that ordinary language was a means to access the world via an association of sense. Riddle-makers have always understood this basic principle of language design and function. Riddles make us both reflect wisely and sometimes laugh at the world, portraying it not as bits and pieces of information but as a cohesive meaning system via metaphor. As Kaivola-Bregenhøj (2016) also emphasizes, no matter what function a riddle may have, lying below its surface is metaphor:

> The degree of metaphor varies in riddles [but] almost every element of a riddle may be metaphorical or consist of an extended metaphor, in which case each line of the metaphor constitutes a new metaphor with a counterpart in the answer part of the riddle.

## Chapter Three

# Poetic Logic

### PROLOGUE

A theoretical framework that can be enlisted to explicate the metaphor hypothesis is the notion of *poetic logic*—a term coined by the Italian philosopher Giambattista Vico (chapter 1) (Bergin and Fisch 1984; Danesi 1993, 2004). It is defined as the source of the universal tendency to perceive a connectivity among things that is expressed in primary (root) metaphors. The latter are the verbal imprints of this connective consciousness. The workings of poetic logic can be seen concretely in how riddles are constructed, as root metaphorical structures, which give an abstract, "unseeable" concept in the answer a specific concrete form. To cite Jean Baudrillard (1987, 7): poetic logic can be defined as the tendency "to produce meaning, to make the world signify, to render it visible." It does so via metaphor.

The notion of poetic logic was introduced by Vico in his landmark treatise of 1725, *The New Science* (Bergin and Fisch 1984). He described it as a universal form of imaginative thinking that allows us to understand the world not as made up of bits and pieces, but as a holistic entity, in which the parts are connected with metaphorical language. The metaphor hypothesis is a more explicit version of poetic logic theory, claiming that nominative speech, which produces labels for things, evolved into language when metaphor appeared onto the evolutionary scene, allowing for the verbal bits and pieces to be blended together to generate consciousness of "invisible" things—*life, yearly cycles*, and the like. Vico maintained, however, that it is not possible to study poetic logic directly, since the mind cannot study itself. So, he suggested that access to it can be gained by examining metaphor. As remarkable as that insight was in the era in which it was put forth, it was largely ignored until the latter part of the twentieth century where it started to spread throughout linguistics, psychology, and anthropology (chapter 1).

The aim of this chapter is to go deeper into the theory of poetic logic, as the source of the root metaphors that undergirded the early riddles and myths. Poetic logic can be explicated simply as the brain's ability to use the senses to link things together into holistic ideas via metaphor. It is this "linking through sense" capacity that makes the human mind unique and powerful. Actually, Vico distinguished between *poetic logic* and *poetic wisdom*. The latter is the capacity to think imaginatively (which Vico called the *fantasia*), rather than rationally, that is, in terms of *mythos*, rather than *lógos*; the former is the ability of the brain to use the *fantasia's* sensory images to create forms of meaning (which Vico called the *ingegno*), such as metaphor. Once these "poetic forms" are created, they become part of both individual and communal memory (*memoria*). In this framework, full-blown language is *memoria*—hence the reason why we can use it easily after its acquisition without having to learn its separate parts over and over. In conceptual metaphor theory, poetic wisdom would be envisioned as the source of images schemas and poetic logic as the neural mechanism that converts these into root metaphors. In effect, poetic wisdom has bestowed upon humans the capacity to imagine abstract and even fictional (context-free) beings, objects, and events. As Verene (1981, 101) has put it, it has allowed humans "to know from the inside" by extending "what is made to appear from sensation beyond the unit of its appearance and to have it enter into connection with all else that is made by the mind from sensation." The "entering into connection with all else" is the function of poetic logic. So, the faculties that underlie the production of metaphor in Vichian terms can be shown diagrammatically as follows:

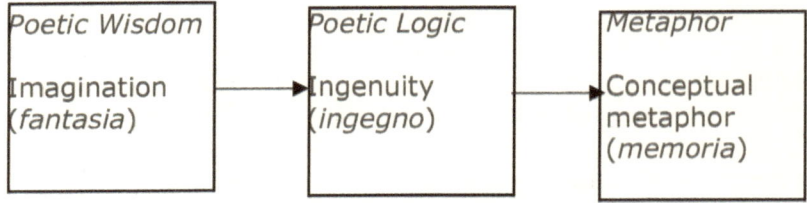

**Figure 3.1 Genesis of Metaphor Based on Vico.**
*Source:* Marcel Danesi

## POETIC LOGIC

The three-part flow model of metaphor described above manifests itself in the creation and comprehension of a riddle, since it involves three states of mind—imagination (poetic wisdom), ingenuity (poetic logic), and memory (metaphor). At first, a riddle presents us with a statement that appears to be either inconsistent, unrealistic, or illogical. To grasp its real (hidden) content, one must use imaginative thinking, which involves connecting the parts in the riddle to each other and to referents beyond it by inference, association, and other connective processes. From this, we might at a certain point see how the parts are connected, tying them together conceptually on the basis of the underlying metaphorical formula on which the riddle is constructed. The metaphorical formula is part of language as a memory system and can thus be rediscovered or fleshed out from the riddle.

All early symbolic-linguistic creations are guided by the same conceptual flow. The *fantasia*, as part of poetic wisdom, is the primary faculty of mind underlying the sense of how things are related to each other and, thus, what they might mean in particular and in general. We use various terms in English to designate this ability, including *intuition, hunch, informed guess*, and so on. The term *poetic wisdom* blends all these together, alluding to a single faculty of mind that involves intuitive foreknowledge of something. The *fantasia* is the main component of this faculty. Poetic logic comes into play when the *ingegno* transforms the intuitive hunches of the imagination into metaphorical mappings, to shed light on some concept or complex abstraction. In effect, poetic logic allows humans to literally "construct" their understanding of the world, interpreting it metaphorically, not just via preprogrammed communicative imprints. Vico expressed this in his well-known *verum-factum* principle—*verum esse ipsum factum* ("truth itself is a fact" or "the truth is made")—well before the advent of conceptual metaphor theory and constructivist models in philosophy and the social sciences. As he put it (Bergin and Fisch 1984, 331), "The world of civil society has certainly been made by men, and its principles are therefore to be found within the modifications of our own human mind."

In effect, metaphor has endowed humans with the ability to transform their hunches, wherever they lack understanding ("the indefinite nature of the human mind," Bergin and Fisch 1984, 120) into specific modes of connective understanding—a process that Charles Peirce (1931–1958, V, 180) called *abduction*:

> The abductive suggestion comes to us like a flash. It is an act of *insight*, although of extremely fallible insight. It is true that the different elements of the hypothesis were in our minds before; but it is the idea of putting together what we had never before dreamed of putting together which flashes the new suggestion before our contemplation.

It is the *ingegno* that converts abductive suggestions into root metaphors and early narrative constructs (such as the Oedipus myth), which in turn form the basis of *memoria* (history):

> For the first indubitable principle posited above is that this world of nations has certainly been made by men, and its guise must therefore be found within the modifications of our own human mind. And history cannot be more certain than when he who creates the things also narrates them (Bergin and Fisch 1984, 349).

This tripartite flow that is purported to characterize phylogeny can clearly be seen in language ontogeny—the origin and development of language in every child. The research in the latter case shows, overall, that children start by making metaphorical hunches about how things are named, and over time and exposure to speech, refining their verbal memory from the specific languages and narratives they have acquired in childhood (Vygotsky 1962). When children describe, say, the "moon" in the sky as a *ball*, we can see the operation of poetic logic in a nutshell: (a) they see a round object for which they do not yet have a name; (b) so they infer that the same name given to another round object, a *ball*, can be mapped onto the one in the sky; and (c) without any adult intervention, the name they devised for the moon will be used again for subsequent naming purposes of objects that share the property of roundness. In this scenario, roundness is the source domain that is mapped onto any target domain that is perceived to possess this property.

Language development, therefore, involves metaphorical and contextualized abductions. As Vygotsky (1962, 298) put it, "The primary word is not a straightforward symbol for a concept but rather an image, a picture, a mental sketch of a short concept, a short tale about it—indeed, a small work of art." The psycholinguists Glucksberg and Danks (1975, 204–205) reached the conclusion that children typically use metaphorical modes of representation because they lack knowledge of the relevant linguistic and societal forms of meaning. By describing a bald father as having *a hole in his head*, a child is using metaphor to fill in a conceptual lacuna via a mapping process. During their first stages of development, children acquire a minimal concrete vocabulary that reflects a need to understand beings, objects, and events in the immediate environment with verbal labels. Children then pass typically through a secondary stage when they make up the labels that they lack via metaphorical processes. The transition from childhood to adulthood occurs when language becomes the basis of thinking about the world.

Poetic logic is the neural faculty that allows children universally to pass from names to metaphors and thus complex thoughts. Its appearance in riddles and myths follows the same pattern. The Riddle of the Sphinx, for instance, (1) is a product of poetic wisdom (imaginative thinking) (2) that connects phases of the day to phases of life (ingenuity) and thus (3) becomes part of language (metaphor) and narrative (the Oedipus myth). Like the child's mappings to fill in gaps of understanding, so too the Sphinx's Riddle fills in a conceptual gap—understanding why life is destined to be what it is.

In this model, the earliest myths are extended metaphorical narratives that correspond ontologically to the early riddles.

Vico elaborated a theory of history (*memoria*) based on a *corso* ("course") that unfolds in three stages, which he called "ages"—the "divine," the "heroic," and the age of "equals." He portrayed each one as manifesting its own particular kind of language and consciousness. So, in the "age of the gods," history is constructed via myths, which are based on root metaphors; in the subsequent "age of heroes," history revolves around certain powerful figures, or cultural heroes, about whom legends are spoken and written. The language used is metonymic (and synecdochic), with heroic themes becoming symbols for cultural values, such as valor in the case of Achilles in the Homeric literature. Finally, in the "age of equals," history is devised as rational and sequential, based on prose forms of language. The *corso* unfolds as shown below:

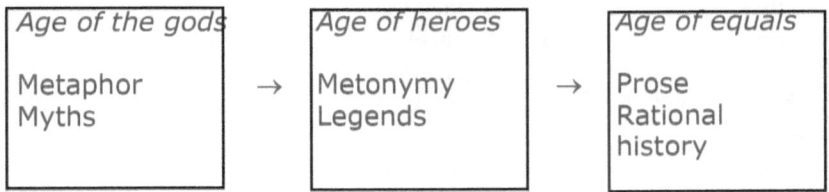

**Figure 3.2 Vico's** *Corso* **of History.**
*Source*: **Marcel Danesi**

The course of memorable history (*memoria*) thus goes from a metaphorical form, through a heroic, metonymic one, to a prosaic-rationalistic one. The first age creates and uses myths (and riddles as claimed here) to understand the world; the second heroic age, uses legends and narratives to represent history in the figure of a particular heroic figure or figures; and the third, rational age, is based on prosaic history and language. Rationality, according to Vico, is humanity's greatest achievement; but human beings do not inherit rationality from their biological legacy, but as the end point of the *corso*, which is iterated in ontogeny, with every child going through the same sequence of "ages" in microcosm. Stripped of culture (*memoria*), human beings would be forced to resort to their poetic wisdom to make sense of the world all over again. Thus, Vico did not see the *corso* as linear and irreversible—he elaborated the idea of the *ricorso*, the return of an earlier age in the life of a culture, whereby poetic wisdom allows humans to reinvent themselves.

As Fletcher (1991, 149) observes, perhaps the most important aspect of poetic logic is that "it identifies *homo sapiens* with *homo faber*—cultural thinking with cultural making." Vico saw *memoria* as the lasting product of poetic logic, given that its metaphorical constructs are "shared by an entire class, an entire people, an entire nation, or the entire human race" (Bergin and Fisch 1984, 142). As Rudolf Arnheim (1969, 233) has observed, in line with the notion of poetic logic, the categories of language have experiential and perceptual origins, not innate grammatical ones, given that "human thinking cannot go beyond the patterns suppliable by the human senses." The imaginative and inventive use of these patterns undergirds the full richness of human language, art, and the other shared expressive systems of humanity. Every new idea or expression is a product of these shared patterns. In the Sphinx's Riddle, for example, the common experience of a day passing through phases is shared by the "entire human race," as corroborated by its appearance in riddles across antiquity (chapter 1). In this way, the riddle is a mini-theory of life based on inference, association, and informed guessing, or abduction (above).

Vico viewed the *fantasia* as the central feature of poetic wisdom, since it allows people universally to sense how things are related to each other and what they might mean in themselves. He sought access to its workings through an etymological-philological study of humanity's first words and myths—to which the *fantasia* gave birth. To this, mythic riddles can certainly be added. The *fantasia* liberates human beings from the constraints imposed on all other organisms by biological imprints. Prefiguring the biologist Jakob von Uexküll (1909), Vico found a constant point of contact between the human body, such as physical vision (the act of seeing with the eyes), and human mental activity, or inner vision (the act of seeing inside the brain). Von Uexküll argued that every species had different inner and outer "visions." In humans the inner visions are produced by the *fantasia*. Intrinsic to the metaphor hypothesis is the finding that the same pattern of inner visions (image schemas) emerges in the earliest riddles across the ancient world, whereby only the specific language changes (its surface form), while its deep metaphorical structure (mapping the image schemas onto the same target domains) remains constant.

## METAPHOR AND POETIC LOGIC

The operation of poetic logic allows us to understand a concept such as *life*, which seems to defy a straightforward explanation or demonstration, via associations, inferences, and hunches with things that are "visible" (as Baudrillard put it) and part of a common understanding. *Life* cannot be "shown" to someone directly, it can only be presented via metaphorical mappings onto things that can actually be seen, such as the three phases of a day.

In the Sphinx's Riddle, the metaphor was, in fact, based on how daytime is perceived in terms of the temporal phases that it presents to experience, perhaps based on the varying intensity of daylight, from morning to evening. Given the open-ended range of the *fantasia*, *life* can be portrayed in many other metaphorical ways, as for example, in terms of the source domain of *stages* (chapter 1). The operation of poetic logic in this case allows us to envision a stage as a locale where life can be shown to an audience through the roles of the characters on the stage, through the actions that unfold on it, and so on and so forth. In so doing, the metaphor entails that we perceive life and stages as suggestive of each other.

The theater itself may, in fact, have come about in order to make life intelligible—it is no coincidence that the Oedipus legend became widely known via various Greek plays. With its characters and plot, the legend is perceived as a source domain through which life can be examined, including the notion of life as a self-fulfilling prophecy based on destiny and character. The theater remains, to this day, an overarching metaphor for life. In any of its modern versions, it puts *life* on display in a concrete and understandable way. The ontological linkage between the two is also the reason why we commonly use theater terms in conversations about life. For example, if we ask someone "What is your life like?" we are likely to get a response such as "My life is a comedy" or "My life is a farce," from which we can draw specific inferences. As will be discussed in the next chapter, these are derived metaphorical frames that extend the underlying root conceptual metaphor. Such *life metaphors* permeate all kinds of discourses as a template for understanding life in its many details, complexities, and vicissitudes. They reveal how we think, how we talk, and why certain things are the way they are. And no special intellectual powers or advanced linguistic training are required to produce or understand such metaphors. Every child is born with the faculty to do so, that is, with the faculty of poetic logic.

The power of poetic logic lies in the fact that it allows people to come up with a common understanding of similar abstractions—*life*, *love*, *destiny*, *cycles*, *nature*, and so on. Indeed, *life* could be mapped by any source domain that would make sense in a specific cultural context, provided that it is exemplary of life in some way. So, for example, a statement such as *life is a river* coined in a culture where rivers play an important role in sustaining life would be "poetically logical" and, thus, highly effective in explaining what life means. While source domains might vary somewhat, it appears that in antiquity some image schemas have archetypal (universal) value and application. The *phases* image schema, for example, appears in riddles across the world, mapped against abstractions such as *time*, *life*, *destiny*, and so on. It is the source of the first root metaphors, which in turn entered into subsequent metaphorical interactions to produce increasingly abstract notions (discussed in chapter 4 as a layering process).

Like Aristotle, Vico saw metaphor as a strategy for explicating or exemplifying abstract notions. And like the Greek philosopher, he claimed that the strategy itself resulted from an association of sense between what is unknown and what is familiar. The association, however, is not just a matter of convenience or expedience. Rather, the two parts of the metaphor suggest each other ontologically. In effect, by saying that *life is a stage*, we are also implying that *stages are life*. This bidirectional system of implications can be called simply "sense implication" (Danesi 2017), meaning that there is a common ground of experiential understanding between the source and target domains that engenders the metaphorical mapping. This commonality of metaphorical understanding is the reason why the folk traditions of early cultures (especially their myths and fables) are understandable across cultures, even if translations may add or subtract from the original language of the stories. The fable, for instance, is usually a tale about metaphorical animals, which are portraits of human personalities. The tale may also be about metaphorical trees, winds, streams, stones, and other natural objects. In all such cases, the same pattern of sense implication will be noted.

Research in conceptual metaphor theory has made it obvious that metaphorical meaning is not an option, but often the only way that a language form can be understood (Kövecses 2020; Zhang, Zhang, Peng, and Jung 2021). The literalist approach to meaning extraction proposes that we encode and decode linguistic messages on the basis of literal meaning first, deciding on a metaphorical one only when a literal interpretation is not possible. But conceptual metaphor theory has brought forward evidence to show why this view is no longer tenable. If contextual information is missing from an utterance such as *The killer is an animal*, our inclination is to interpret it metaphorically, not literally (chapter 1). Only if we are told that the *killer* is an actual "animal" (a bear, a cougar, etc.) would a literal interpretation come to mind. And even in this case, the use of the term *killer* is inherently metaphorical, since it indicates that we interpret actions of other animals in human terms.

Now, the question becomes: Is all language metaphorical? As Vico himself argued, metaphor is found at the beginning of language, that is, when naming or conceptualizing something unknown concretely. In later stages of understanding, metonymy, synecdoche, and irony emerge as supplementary modes of thought and language. So, while rhetorical tropes remain distinctive, and play key roles in different aspects of discourse, the approach to metaphor in both Vico and conceptual metaphor theory is that it is the core meaning-making faculty behind conceptual language. Some of the traditional rhetorical tropes are thus seen as manifestations of metaphorical reasoning, rather than as separate forms of language. For example, personification (*My cat speaks Italian*, *Mystery resides here*) is viewed as a specific kind of conceptual metaphor, in which *people* is the source domain that is mapped onto animals, events, and other target domains.

There are a few caveats that must be taken into account vis-à-vis conceptual metaphor theory. First, whether or not all abstract concepts are structured metaphorically is an open question. When we generalize adjectives into nouns—*great* → *greatness*, *beautiful* → *beauty*—the abstractive process may not easily fit into the conceptual metaphor framework, although it could be argued that these too are mappings from a concrete qualitative (adjectival) source domain onto an abstract (nounal) target domain, but this might be a somewhat artificial explanation. Despite such cautions, the current research within conceptual metaphor theory has made it no longer tenable to assign metaphorical meaning to some subordinate category vis-à-vis literal meaning.

But, then, the foregoing discussion seems to be a highly reductive one—that is, it seems to reduce the mind to metaphor. Actually, as mentioned, there is a flow in the mind that goes from poetic wisdom to metaphor via poetic logic, which is hardly a reductive model of mind. It suggests that the key faculty of mind is the *fantasia* and that metaphor is the initial way in which the abductions made by the imagination are given linguistic form. The debate on the nature of mind goes back to antiquity. Plato, for instance, saw ideas as separate from the biology of the senses (for example, Plato 2013). The circle, he claimed, is something that exists within the confines of the mind, given that it can be found nowhere in Nature as such. Thus, if the concept of the circle cannot be induced from sensory observation, then it must be innate. Descartes (1637) reinforced Plato's theory of innate ideas, also claiming that the mind was separate from the body. Vico was among the first to challenge the Platonic-Cartesian view because it told us nothing about how we invent words for supposed innate notions such as *circles* in the first place. The names we give to things, and the ways in which we construct our concepts, are typically the result of experiential mappings—indeed, the occurrence of ring-like structures and patterns in the world are encapsulated in the single word *circle*, which gathers these tokens into itself as a typological sign. This tokens-to-type process is found in thought-naming systems. The ancient names of the gods, for instance, were humanity's first metaphors for explaining natural events. As discussed (chapter 1), *Jove* was a metaphor for the thundering sky, given human form so that it could be understood concretely—that is, as a father figure who punishes his children by throwing bolts at them to vent his anger. Once the sky was called *Jove*, all other experiences of the same phenomenon could be "found again" in the name, much like the vignette above of children using *ball* to name any round object. *Jove* is a metaphorical separation of the sky from the earth, of the divine from the human world. From these metaphorical ideas, the first conscious humans learned to make sense together.

Universal ideas do indeed exist, as Plato assumed, but they seem to have a different source—they are based on poetic logic. It is the source of concepts such as *life is a journey*, which is found virtually everywhere, not as an innate Platonic idea, but as a creation of poetic logic on a common ground of experiential understanding. This is why the *journey* metaphor is found in literary traditions across time. In the Middle Ages, the Italian poet Dante showed in his *Divine Comedy* (1307) that understanding life involves a journey through hell, purgatory, and heaven. Interestingly, as in the Riddle of the Sphinx, the journey unfolds in terms of three dimensions, perhaps indicating that "threeness" is itself a root source domain that can be mapped in an infinitude of ways to understand intangible phenomena.

Poetic logic is not limited to poets and riddle-makers. It is constantly operative. As a practical example of how poetic logic might guide our choice of words during a thought pattern or conversational event, let us assume hypothetically that someone is not feeling well and that it is raining at the same time. The person sees the rain dripping down a window. That sight will probably impel the individual to associate the droplets of rain to their emotional state. Now, it is this association that will tend to manifest itself in any discourse that the person will produce for some specific reason. For example, if someone were to ask the individual how they felt at that moment, the person might say something such as *I'm feeling drippy today*. The choice of the word *drippy* is a trace to both the individual's mood and the outside weather, given the context in which it was uttered. As it turns out, the expression is an instantiation of a conceptual metaphor—*mood is a meteorological state*. The same thought formula is the source of expressions such as *I'm under the weather today*, *The skies are shining on their lives*, and so on. We rarely recognize the presence of such thought formulas in our communications because, over time, they have become discourse habits and thus unconscious.

## CONSCIOUSNESS AND COGNITION

The notions of poetic wisdom and poetic logic provide a framework for concretely discussing several key aspects of conceptual metaphor theory. One of these is event structure, or a dependency between events, some of which can only occur or be performed in a sequence and some of which might be co-occurrent. In conceptual metaphor theory, the key notion is that the dependency or co-occurrence of events is expressed metaphorically, showing little variation as to the source domains used to conceptualize them. In the

Riddle of the Sphinx, for example, the two events are *life* and *day phases*. The mapping of the *phases* source domain onto life is not only found across many languages, but it displays the same pattern of what Lakoff and Johnson (1980) call *invariance*, whereby the metaphor maps the relevant component of meaning (sequential phases) from the source domain that remains coherent in the target domain (life phases)—that is, the mapping preserves the basic event structure. Lakoff (1979, 215) defines the invariance principle as "metaphorical mappings preserve the cognitive topology (that is, the image-schema structure) of the source domain, in a way consistent with the inherent structure of the target domain."

Utilizing Vichian theory, it can be said that the sense that two events are connected, via invariance, is part of poetic wisdom, the capacity to envision "basic" connections among things—an awareness that defines a rudimentary form of consciousness, shaped by metaphor (Glicksohn 2001). According to Jaynes (1976, 66), there may well be no consciousness without metaphor to give it a form:

> The conscious mind is a spatial analog of the world and mental acts are analogs of bodily acts. Consciousness operates only on objectively observable things. Or, to say it another way with echoes of John Locke, there is nothing in consciousness that is not an analog of something that was in behavior first.

It is poetic logic that establishes the invariance meaning pattern between the events via metaphor. Once this occurs, awareness of the invariance through language crystallizes. It is no longer part of a raw consciousness but becomes constrained linguistically to produce a cognitive state—understanding through language. To put it in neuropsychological terms, consciousness is a function of the right hemisphere, where metaphor originates, and cognition is a function of the left hemisphere, where language resides. This shift from right-to-left can be called bimodality (Danesi 2003), in contrast to bicamerality, which, as Jaynes (1976) has argued, eventually broke down so that the hemispheres could become specialized. Bimodality implies that the brain takes in unfamiliar information (of which it becomes consciously aware) via the experiential (probing) right-hemisphere, where metaphors and analogies crystallize; it then transfers these to the left hemisphere where the event structure is given specific linguistic form, producing thought (cognition) in the more specific sense. The end result is semantics, the system of meanings that are part of language memory. At this point, language and cognition are one and the same, as some linguists have maintained (for instance, Sapir 1921; Whorf 1956). When this occurs, the semantic system of a language is established in its core. The Sphinx's Riddle charts in microcosm how we proceed

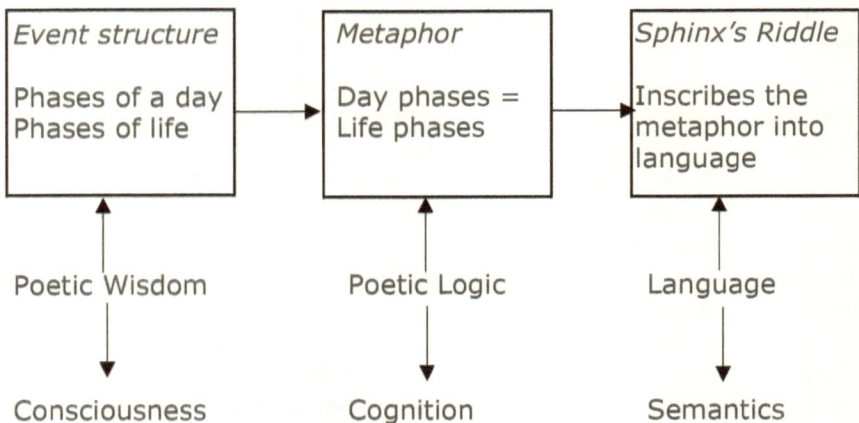

**Figure 3.3 A Poetic Logic Model of the Riddle of the Sphinx.**
*Source*: **Marcel Danesi**

from a poetic form of the consciousness of dependent (invariant) events to their imprinting in metaphorical language via poetic logic (see Figure 3.3).

Poetic logic is what transforms the awareness of event structure into cognition via metaphor—in a phrase, it converts a consciousness of things into metaphorical language. Making sense is a product of poetic logic producing the first image schemas. Early people devised riddles and made-up stories about gods in the sky who interacted with humans—whereby human events were imagined in terms of divine events. From these came the first image schemas of the world. Poetic logic is the faculty that makes these images part of the very structure of the human brain.

As literary historian Northrop Frye (1981, 1990) also observed, the Vichian paradigm provides key insights into how consciousness became thought via images (more specifically image schemas in conceptual metaphor theory). As he (1990, xxii–xxiii) put it, the construction of mind results from "the images of higher and lower, the categories of beauty and ugliness, the feelings of love and hatred, the associations of sense experience, [that] can be expressed only by metaphor and yet cannot be either dismissed or reduced to projections of something else . . . its presence gives a very different appearance to many elements of human life, including religion, which depend on metaphor but do not become less 'real' or 'true' by doing so."

As metaphorically shaped cognition develops into subsequent stages of language, the result is an explicit (cognitive) understanding of what things mean, since they now can be described and discussed with language (Honeck and Hoffman 1980). This is the role of *memoria*, as discussed, which constitutes a semantic repertoire of forms that allows for the construction or reconstruction of meaning.

In sum, the gist of the foregoing discussion is that the flow from consciousness to cognition is shaped by metaphor. The neuronal structures involved in this flow are spread widely throughout the brain, primarily by neurotransmitters, but the right-to-left modal flow is emerging as a neuropsychological pattern, which also enlists the limbic system in the processing of language (Damasio 1994). In effect, all the parts of the brain work in tandem to produce thought—which is encoded in linguistic forms.

## FRAMING THE METAPHOR HYPOTHESIS

The forgoing discussion allows for a Vichian framing of the metaphor hypothesis—namely, riddles reveal how poetic logic works to transform consciousness of the structure of events via metaphor, which then becomes the basis of the semantic system of language and its attendant cognition. As contemporary research in cognitive science has shown, some of which has been discussed in this chapter, this is hardly just speculation, but seemingly a verity about how we think through language and because of language. Metaphor is a verbal trace to how poetic logic brings about language cognition.

This is why Vico called the first speakers "poets," since they resorted to metaphor to come to grips with their consciousness of events in the world, producing early culture based on stories of the gods and their dominion over humans. These allowed early people to partition the phenomena of the world, organize them cognitively, classify them, and explain them as metaphysical events. Thus the early institutions, laws, cultural rituals, and the like result from poetic logic. The metaphor hypothesis is, in effect, a contemporary way of saying that poetic logic is the originating force of language and cognition, as opposed to speech as a set of signals for referring to things directly—a force that (as mentioned) manifests itself early in childhood language and cognitive development. Vico himself saw children's language as reflective of how language would have evolved in the species (Bergin and Fisch 1984, 204–210, 403, 809, 933–934). As he put it, what will eventually become an abstract concept is formed as a metaphor (as we saw with the use of metaphor as a lexical gap-filling strategy in children). The first abstract concepts were formed in an identical way. For instance, the ancient Greeks could only come to grasp the concept of *valor* through the character of Achilles, which was its personified metaphor (Bergin and Fisch 1984, 403). The metaphors of children and early humans are the forms for connecting events that are sensed to be meaningful in human life but which cannot be grasped literally (states, causes, changes, difficulties, purposes, obstacles, achievements, and so on). The nature of the connections between things, universal and particular, is not available to cognition at first. They can only be imagined in terms of a poetic wisdom (consciousness). But they are not merely fanciful nor principally subjective. They are real connections made in imaginative form. Myths, therefore, always state perceived truths—as do riddles. Cognition, on the other hand, requires that the story to be told display a coherent order of the conceptual material enlisted. As Vico put it, "the first founders of humanity applied themselves to sensory topics, by which they brought together those properties or qualities or relations of individuals and species which were, so to speak, concrete, and created from poetic genera" (Bergin and Fisch 1984, 495). Children produce metaphors regularly in order to express the resemblance between objects and events that they sense intuitively (Gibbs 2017; Kövecses 2020). The same type of resemblance detection via metaphor can be seen in the early riddles and myths, all of which suggest that metaphor is indeed an originating force in transforming consciousness into cognition.

## THE SENSE IMPLICATION HYPOTHESIS

A question that arises from any discussion of the metaphor hypothesis, as it relates to poetic logic, is the following one: What actual neural mechanism produces the shift from intuitions about the invariant structure of events into metaphor? In current cognitive science that mechanism is called *blending* (Turner 1997; Fauconnier and Turner 2002). According to this theory, the parts of a metaphor are located in different "mental spaces," which are blended together via a mapping process. Blending goes on constantly as people think and talk, activating groups of neurons in different spaces that are mapped onto each other as guided by context.

Without going into specifics here, blending does not actually aim to explain how sensed event structures become thoughts via metaphor directly; it explains how metaphor is formed in the brain via the co-activation of different spaces within it that carry specific kinds of information. As Raymond Gibbs (2000) has remarked, blending theory is not a theory as such, but rather a framework for characterizing how metaphor arises in the brain. Another possible framework is the notion of *sense implication*, or the idea that different referents are connected via metaphor because they implicate each other conceptually (Sebeok and Danesi 2000). As an example of how sense implication might operate, consider the word *blue* in English. As a concrete concept, the word *blue* was probably coined by observing a pattern of hue found in natural phenomena such as the sky and the sea, and then noting the occurrence of the same hue in other things, to which the same word is applied.

The specific image of *blue* that comes to mind will, of course, be different from individual to individual. But all images will fall within a certain hue range on the light spectrum. In a phrase, the word *blue* allows speakers of English to talk and think about the occurrence of a specific color in a concrete way. But that is not all it does. Speakers use the very same concept to characterize emotions, morals, and other abstractions. Consider, for instance, the two sentences below:

> On a rainy day I always get the *blues*.
> The news hit me right out of the *blue*.

The use of *blues* in the first expression to mean "sad" or "gloomy" is the result of a culture-specific sense-implication process, coming out of the tradition of blues music, which is felt typically to evoke sadness or melancholy through its melodies, harmonies, rhythms, and lyrics. The use of *blue* in the second expression to render the concept of "unexpectedness" comes, instead, out of the tradition of ascribing unpredictability to the weather, symbolized by a *blue sky*. Upon closer examination, such uses belong to situation-specific metaphorical traditions, which are nonetheless based on root source domains—the former is an instantiation of the conceptual metaphor that connects *mood* with *color* and the latter of the conceptual metaphor that connects *destiny* with *Nature*, which literary critics classify under the rubric of *pathetic fallacy*. These two sense linkages underlie the conceptual structure of the above two sentences and, indeed, of many other common expressions such as the following:

> She turned *red* with embarrassment.
> My cousin is *green* with envy.
> I heard it from an *angry wind*.
> *Cruel clouds* are gathering over the world.

Examples such as these show that the source and target domains implicate each other through an entailment based on sense. As anthropologist Roger Wescott (1980) has amply documented, color vocabularies seem in fact to have originated through such entailment, that is, through an association of hues with natural and human events. In the ancient Hittite language, for instance, words for colors initially designated plants and trees; in Hebrew, the name of the first man, *Adam*, meant *red* and *alive*, and still today, in languages of the Slavic family, *red* signifies *living* and *beautiful*. In effect, Wescott showed that in many languages (perhaps in most) the names for colors were forged as phenomenological metaphors—a tendency that is still manifest in how we label certain emotions to this day: for example, *tickled pink*, which alludes to the face turning pink with laughter and so on and so forth.

Consider, more specifically, the color *red*, which is associated with "blood" and "vitality." In many languages, the naming of "red" co-occurred with the naming of "blood," leaving a residue in many symbolic practices. In some group rituals, for instance, it is common to slit the wrists of fellow members and rub them together so that they may become *blood brothers*. In the medieval ages, it was commonly believed that love was a sickness that could be cured by bleeding people. Such examples provide anecdotal evidence that metaphor, symbols, and rituals are linked through the same pattern of source domains.

The sense implication hypothesis provides a plausible explanation for a host of semantic subtleties that would otherwise go unexplained. Take, for example the *people are animals* conceptual metaphor (chapter 1). Consider further the choice of *snake* from the *animal* source domain: for example, *John is a snake*. This particular choice produces a specific type of semantic system of personality that portrays *John* as a serpentine animal in general. However, if we want to change our metaphorical portrait, then we can construct derivative metaphorical concepts that allow us to zero in on specific details of personality:

> He's a *cobra*.
> He's a *viper*.
> He is a *boa constrictor*.

In so doing, we are thus able to modulate our descriptions of personality in ways that parallel sensory reactions (or culturally shaped perceptions) to each type of snake. This suggests that source domains are themselves based on a sense implication process—so, the target domain of *personality* implicates a specific kind of source domain *(animals),* which, in turn, implicates specific subdomains (types of animals) which, in their turn, suggest other subdomains (types of snake), and so on. The domains are linked through sense implication.

Sense implication allows us, overall, to correlate physical affective processes to conceptual ones by suggesting that they entail each other—a position that has been adopted broadly ever since the advent of conceptual metaphor theory, although not specified as such (Lakoff 1987; Johnson 1987). Consider the concept of *anger*. Because anger entails certain specific kinds of bodily reactions, such as an increase in muscle tension, our conceptualization of *anger* will implicate these very reactions—*bodily temperature, redness*, and so on—in some physical way and to some degree. This is why concepts such as *boiling*, *redness*, and so on are used in metaphorical expressions to deliver the concept of *anger*:

> I'm *boiling* with anger.
> Don't be so angry; you're face is *red*.

In such cases the implication is sensory. However, in others it can be intellectual. Consider, as an example, the metaphorical uses of the word *house*. As a concrete concept, the word denotes "any (free-standing) structure intended for human habitation." This meaning can be seen in utterances such as *I bought a new house yesterday*, *House prices are continually going up in this city*, *We repainted our house the other day*, and so on. Now, when *house* is used as a source domain it is perceived as a *container* image schema—that is, a "container of human beings." It is this image schema that is mapped onto the following meanings:

> The *house* is in session (*a legislature*).
> The *house* roared with laughter (*an audience*).
> They sleep at one of the *houses* at Harvard (*dormitory*).

The *house* concept can, in effect, be used to refer to anything that implicates humans coming together in some "container" for some specific reason; that is, audiences, legislative assemblies, and dormitories imply "container structures" that humans can be said to occupy in some metaphorical way.

Sense implication is, in the end, guided by poetic wisdom and thus by the *fantasia*. The American philosopher Susanne Langer (1948, 129) compared it, appropriately, to a "fantasy":

> Suppose a person sees, for the first time in his life, a train arriving at a station. He probably carries away what we should call a "general impression" of noise and mass. Very possibly he has not noticed the wheels going round, but only the rods moving like a runner's knees. He does not instantly distinguish smoke from steam, nor the hissing from the squeaking. Yet the next time he watches a train pull in the process is familiar. His mind retains a fantasy which "means" the general concept, "a train arriving at a station." Everything that happens the second time is, to him like or unlike the first time. The fantasy . . . was abstracted from the very first instance, and made the later ones "familiar."

## METAPHOR AND GRAMMAR

A key question that the foregoing discussion raises is the following: Where does the emergence of grammar fit into paradigms such as the blending and sense implication ones? It is useful to enlist the notions of *deep* and *surface structure* in order to provide a tentative answer to this question. These are associated primarily with early generative grammar (Chomsky 1957, 1965). In that model, the deep structure contains universal rules of syntax that are converted via language-specific transformational rules into grammar-specific surface structures. But in terms of the metaphor hypothesis, it can be said that the deep structure is not syntactic, but rather based on source domains and their attendant image schemas, which are converted into grammatical forms in the surface structure via metaphor. So, the grammatical layout of the Riddle of the Sphinx involves an image schematic deep structure based on *phases* that is mapped onto the riddle as a question that itself is organized sequentially in terms of the dependent phases—hence the order of *dawn-noon-twilight*. Therefore, within conceptual metaphor theory, the words that are assigned to particular constructional slots indicate the event structure of the source domain, and words in other slots represent the metaphor's target domain. For example, as Sullivan (2007, 1–3) states vis-à-vis a metaphorical expression such as *bright idea*, the mapping from the deep to the surface involves "the source-domain predicating the adjective *bright* (metaphorically meaning "intelligent") so as to modify the target domain of *idea*. A similar phrase with a target-domain adjective and a source-domain noun, such as *intelligent light*, which bears the meaning "intelligent idea." In non-metaphoric constructions, conceptually autonomous elements are used in syntactic slots to elaborate the meaning of conceptually dependent elements. In metaphoric constructions, the elaboration process involves the placement of a target domain in such a way that impels us to interpret the dependent elements metaphorically.

Vico gives an interesting and parallel account of how grammar might have come into existence. The first words, he claims, were formed by imitation, that is, primarily through sound modeling "which we still find in children happily expressing themselves" (Bergin and Fisch 1984, 447). This is the function of primordial speech (discussed in chapter 5). As Tsur (1992) has also demonstrated, this is how sense implication works at a primordial level of speech. Then came interjections, "which are sounds articulated under the impetus of violent passions" (Bergin and Fisch 1984, 448). Under the impulse of the passions a sequence of word categories came into being. Pronouns came after the interjections because they served to help us share "our ideas with others concerning things which we cannot name or whose names another may not understand" (Bergin and Fisch 1984, 450). Particles with their nouns and finally verbs complete the Vichian phylogenetic sequence of grammar:

> Last of all, the authors of the languages formed the verbs, as we observe children expressing nouns and particles but leaving the verbs to be understood. For

nouns awaken ideas which leave firm traces; particles signifying modifications, do the same; but verbs signify motions, which involve past and future, which are measured from the indivisible present (Bergin and Fisch 1984: 453).

What this scenario suggests is the notion that the parts of speech are interrelated via sense implication, and connected in terms of event structure. Overall, the sense implication paradigm suggests that the parts of speech are dependent upon source domains. Take, as an example, the use of the English prepositions *since* and *for* in sentences such as the following:

> I have been living in this town *since* 2020.
> I have known my new friend *since* November.
> I have not been able to sleep *since* Monday.
> I have lived in that city previously *for* seven years.
> I have known my work colleague *for* nine months.
> I have not been able to sleep *for* seven days.

The complements that follow *since* are, conceptually, *points in time*; that is, they are complements that are parts of a source domain that underlies the conceptual metaphor *time is a point on a line* on which specific years, months, and so on can be shown: *2020, November, Monday*. Complements that follow *for*, on the other hand, are parts of a source domain that underlies the conceptual metaphor *time is a quantity*. This is why they refer to things that can be counted—*seven years, nine months, seven days*. This type of analysis suggests that different metaphorical conceptualizations of *time* in English are mapped directly into the parts of speech. Simply put, the choice of *since* or *for* is governed by a conceptual distinction in the deep structure, not by any abstract rule of grammar. The two dimensions—the metaphorical and the grammatical—are reflexes of each other.

Consider, as another example, the use of *snake* as an instantiation of the conceptual metaphor *people are animals*. In specific sentences, it can show up as a verb if it is the snake's movements that are implicated, or as an adjective, if it is a quality of the snake that is implicated instead:

> He *snaked* his way around the issue.
> She has a *snaky* way of doing things.

The selection of a verb form in the first expression represents the movement of snakes in the portrayal of personality while in the adjectival form it is a serpentine quality of character that is mapped onto the surface grammar. Differences in word order, too, can be traced to deep structure source domains. In Italian, for instance, the difference between the literal and metaphorical meaning of an adjectival concept is often reflected by the different position of the adjective in a noun phrase:

> Lui è un uomo *povero* ("He's an indigent man").
> Lui è un *povero* uomo ("He's a forlorn man").

In the first expression it is the literal meaning of *povero* that is represented in the noun phrase by the post-positioning of the adjective with respect to the noun. In the second, the metaphorical meaning of *povero* is brought out by means of its pre-positioning with respect to the noun, alerting the interlocutor in an anticipatory fashion to this meaning.

A similar approach to grammar is the one formulated by Ronald Langacker (1987, 1990, 1999), who has cogently shown how metaphorical meaning and grammar are intrinsically intertwined. For instance, nouns encode the image schema of a *region* in mind-space. So, a count noun such as *leaf* is envisioned in our minds as referring to something that encircles a *bounded region* and a mass noun such as *water* a *non-bounded region*. Now, this difference in image schematic structure is mapped onto grammatical distinctions. Thus, because *bounded* referents can be counted, the form *leaf* has a corresponding plural form *leaves*, but *water* does not (unless it is used metaphorically as in *the waters of Babylon*). Moreover *leaf* can be preceded by an indefinite article (*a leaf*), *water* cannot. But even before Langacker's work, Rudolf Arnheim (1969, 239–242) presented a similar argument, seemingly explaining the origin of particles such as prepositions and conjunctions in a Vichian style:

> I referred in an earlier chapter to the barrier character of "but," quite different from "although," which does not stop the flow of action but merely burdens it with a complication. Causal relations . . . are directly perceivable actions; therefore "because" introduces an effectuating agent, which pushes things along. How different is the victorious overcoming of a hurdle conjured up by "in spite of" from the displacement in "either-or" or "instead"; and how different is the stable attachment of "with" or "of" from the belligerent "against."

Arnheim (1969, 244) also saw syntax as a "conserving and stabilizing" feature that "also tends to make cognition static and immobile." Syntax allows us to organize our "statements about an intuitively perceived situation and can serve to reconstruct that situation" (Arnheim 1969, 247). It can be said more pertinently with regard to conceptual metaphor theory that prepositions are actually based on specific image schemas. English speakers say that they read something *in a newspaper*, implying through the preposition *in* that the newspaper is imagined as a container of information *into which* one must go to *seek it out*. That is why speakers also say that they *got a lot out of the newspaper*, or that there *was nothing in it*. On the other hand, Italian speakers use the preposition *su* ("on"), implying that the information is impressed on the surface of the pages. Therefore, there are no expressions similar to *we got a lot out of the newspaper* and *there was nothing in it*, because the source domain in the Italian case is that of a writing surface on which information is inscribed.

The use of sense implication to produce various types and levels of concepts that become parts of speech can be called *layering* (Danesi 2001), to be discussed in the next chapter. Suffice it to say here that it allows us to analyze concepts as belonging to different levels or layers of metaphorical cognition. A first-order layer is one that is constructed with concrete source domains (that is, with vehicles referring to concrete referents)—a construction that produces the most basic kind of conceptual metaphor, such as *thinking is seeing*. A second-order layer is one that is derived from first-order concepts. Expressions such as *think up*, *think through*, and so on, are second-order concepts since they result from the linkage of two concepts—*thinking is seeing + ideas are objects*. (Discussed in the next chapter.) The third-order metaphorical layer crystallizes from sense implications of previously formed layers. It is a productive source of cultural symbolism, as will be discussed. For example, in order to understand the meaning of the *rose* as symbolic of *love*, we must first know that it comes from conceptual metaphors such as *love is a plant* (as in *Love grows* and *My love has deep roots*) and *love is sweet* (as in *She's my sweetheart* and *They're on a honeymoon*). The layering of these conceptual metaphors produces *love is a rose,* since a *rose* is both a *plant* and gives off a *sweet* odor.

## EPILOGUE

The overall argument of this chapter has been that the notion of poetic logic is a key one for explicating the metaphor hypothesis, given that it posits a passage from poetic wisdom (*fantasia*) to poetic logic (*ingegno*) to language (*memoria*). Riddles and myths are the first verbal artifacts that document this passage. As riddling evolved to subserve different social-discursive functions (delectation, literary aesthetics, pedagogy), the metaphorical substratum on which the early riddles were implanted, broadened to include various other cognitive modalities.

For Vico, the appearance of metaphor on the evolutionary timetable of humanity made possible the passage from instinctual responses to the world to an abstract and complex form of thinking that transformed sensorial inputs into cognitively usable models of experience via metaphor. The notion of poetic logic thus allows for an examination of the early riddles in terms of a tripartite flow of understanding: poetic wisdom → poetic logic → metaphor.

The shift from poetic logic to metaphor can be explained in several contemporary ways, of which blending and sense implication are but two such ways.

Poetic logic implies that the brain's ability to form images of the world—rendering it "visible," to quote Baudrillard again—has allowed humans to give the imagination a form (via metaphor) that remains memorable and meaningful. As Cicero (1942, 274) so aptly put it, metaphor transforms the senses into a form of inner sensation or inner vision (chapter 1).

Without metaphor, history as a comprehensive form of *memoria* would be impossible. Research on animals has shown that many species can make references to physical reality beyond the instincts. But only human beings have the capacity to transform the nonreflective behavior that they share with the other animals into a reflective one. The distinguishing feature of human *memoria* is, arguably, that it allows humans to imagine the world beyond the instincts via metaphorical structures, such as mythic narratives. Poetic wisdom underlies the innate capacity to do so, while poetic logic is the mechanism that gives metaphorical form to this capacity. Riddles and early myths are concrete evidence of how poetic logic allows us to generate abstract thoughts and complex thinking.

*Chapter Four*

# Riddles and Conceptual Metaphors

**PROLOGUE**

As discussed throughout this book, the Riddle of the Sphinx emerges at the dawn of human history as a prototypical model of how metaphor works in shaping consciousness into linguistic cognition. By mapping the phases of a day against the phases of life, the Sphinx's Riddle illustrates concretely how metaphor transforms an inference into an idea via poetic logic (chapter 3). The *phases* metaphor, moreover, is suggestive of a *journey* image schema, thus creating a linkage that involves a "layering" of metaphors to produce higher levels of abstraction and understanding. It is this layering that gives the Oedipus narrative resonance, which is mirrored in the riddle:

- *Infancy: the dawn of life:* As an infant, Oedipus is left to die on a mountain by Laius, his own father, after the Oracle at Delphi prophesied that he would be killed by his own son.
- *Maturity: the midday of life.* As a young man, Oedipus became aware of the ominous prophecy and decided to go to Thebes to escape it.
- *Old age: the twilight of life.* When Oedipus discovers the truth, which he did not anticipate, he becomes powerless and despondent, blinding himself to the truth.

The earliest riddles across the world had the same layering structure of the Sphinx's Riddle, being connected to concomitant mythic stories (Taylor 1948, 1951; Rickman 2004). Since ancient cultures were unlikely to be in contact, and since they spoke different languages, the implication is that the mythic riddles are also among the earliest evidence of the existence of archetypes in the human brain—archetypes that can be seen to have metaphorical structure.

The goal of this chapter is to refine the metaphor hypothesis in terms of conceptual metaphor theory. To reiterate, in this book, the term *speech* is constrained to designate the ability to name things in the world, while *language* is used to define the ability to combine names into complex thoughts via metaphor. Riddles are among the earliest artifacts that show how this ability emerged. The metaphor hypothesis is in line with the notion of *bicameral mentality*, first formulated by Julian Jaynes (1976), whereby the prelinguistic mind produced an early form of consciousness via the operation of two brain chambers, with one perceived to be speaking and the other listening, eventually leading to a specialization of the two chambers into *hemispheres*—to be discussed in the next chapter, given that there is solid neuroscientific evidence that metaphor has a right-hemispheric locus, while naming in the strictly referential (denotative) sense has a left-hemispheric one. While bicameral theory has been critiqued from several angles, what is relevant here is that it provides a putative framework for relating speech to language via metaphor—a model of origins to which Jaynes himself subscribed.

As discussed throughout this book as well, metaphor also has a naming function as a metaphorical lexical gap filler (Faizullina, Zamaletdinov, and Fattakhova 2020), which has been called phenomenological. But unlike early nominative speech, which involves devising names for referents directly, metaphorical gap filling involves the use of image schemas to do so, as will also be discussed in the final chapter. In effect, a metaphorical name is a mapping of a known source domain onto an unnamed (or unknown) target domain. This phenomenon is common in childhood, as discussed in the previous chapter—lacking a name for the "moon," the child utilizes the word *ball*, acquired in a different context—to name it. The child mapped the property of roundness associated with the word *ball* onto the "moon," because it clearly was perceived by the child as sharing this property. To paraphrase Jakobson and Halle (1956, 91), a phenomenological metaphor arises via a sensed similarity between what it names and what has already been named—in line with sense implication theory. Jakobson (1960) designated such metaphors as evidence of how iconicity (resemblance between referents) is embedded as a propensity in creative language.

Riddles can also be constructed via a blend of metaphor and metonymy. Recall the *face is the person* metonym, which surfaces in all kinds of riddle traditions and cultural practices (chapter 2). While it does have metonymic meaning, a part (*face*) standing for the whole (*person*), its mapping structure still qualifies it as a conceptual metaphor—*source domain:* face → *target domain*: human personality. Similar blends of the two tropes, with virtually identical mappings, are found throughout riddle and narrative traditions, constituting the most plausible reason why the ancient stories (myths, fables, and folktales) that are told throughout the world, are understood in the same ways by all humans, via translation, irrespective of language, culture, or epoch.

This chapter will examine how conceptual metaphor theory allows for a refinement of the metaphor hypothesis, given that the same pattern of conceptual metaphors, such as *the year unfolds in the form of a wheel*, is found in riddles and myths across Europe and Asia—perhaps indicating that the invention of the wheel made life easier throughout the year. As mentioned, a Sanskrit riddle describes a twelve-spoked wheel on which stand 720 sons of one birth alluding to the twelve months of the year, which together have 360 days and 360 nights (Tupper 1903, 102), also perhaps revealing the belief that human life and astronomical processes are intrinsically intertwined. The examination will also constitute, conversely and reciprocally, a field laboratory for validating conceptual metaphor theory. Lakoff (1979) and other cognitive linguists have made the claim that conceptual language originates in metaphor. Examining riddles can provide a concrete means of testing this premise.

## MAPPINGS

To reiterate here, a conceptual metaphor in cognitive linguistics is seen as a thought-form that displays metaphorical structure, whereby domains of reference are mapped onto each other guided by the experience of resemblances or various types of ontological connections among them. So, in the Sphinx's Riddle, the domains are *life* and *days*. Their linkage is guided by imagining the two domains as one conceptual entity. The claim has even been made that this type of mapping corresponds to neural mappings (Feldman and Narayanan 2004; Castel 2015). Whether this is sustainable or not, it is clear that there is a neural basis to the mapping process, given the distribution of the same conceptual metaphors across cultures—that is, while the actual metaphorical expressions vary according to surface grammar and lexicon, they share the same metaphorical deep structure. Below is a schematic diagram illustrating the mappings involved in the *years as a wheel* and the *life unfolds in phases* riddles (discussed in this book) (see Figure 4.1).

A mapping describes how the experience of one domain is the source of understanding for another domain. The point here is that the mappings above appeared (seemingly for the first time) in riddles and myths. In the former the mapping produces a dialectic (literally, a question-and-answer structure); in the latter it produces a narrative. Now, as the conceptual metaphor of *life unfolds in phases* imprints itself into the language—grammar and

86                                   *Chapter Four*

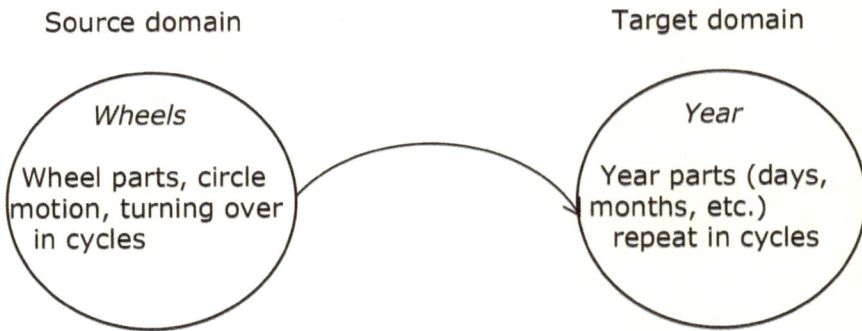

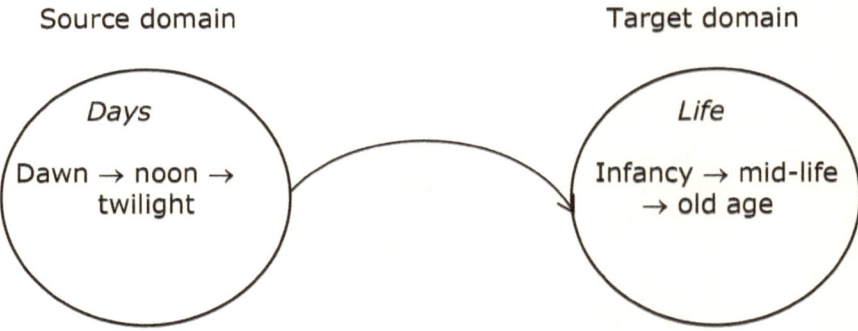

**Figure 4.1 Riddle Mappings.**
*Source:* **Marcel Danesi**

semantics—a process of converting deep metaphorical structure into surface linguistic structure (chapter 3) becomes itself a further mapping process, producing derivative metaphors such as *My life is just beginning*, *My life is at mid-point*, or *My life is in its final stages*. Each particular metaphorical framing of the root metaphor extends the event structure into other domains.

Research in conceptual metaphor theory has shown that mappings are systematic, not exceptional, mechanisms, occurring across all languages (Gibbs 2017; Kövecses 2020). Only the specific source domain involved may vary in non-root, situation-specific metaphors. So, for example, the conceptual metaphor of *thinking is seeing* (*I see your point, I view the matter differently*) is found across the world and is thus easily translatable because it is a root metaphor; on the other hand the conceptual metaphor *ideas are money* (*You cannot put a price on that idea, That notion is worthless*, and so on) is found in specific cultures. But even so, it constitutes a situation-specific manifestation of a deeper root metaphor: *ideas are objects* (in this case with monetary value).

Metaphorical mappings are not limited to language. Depicting people as animals in the artistic and narrative domains is a product of the same process. This is why stories for children focusing on human personality via animal characters or why mythic stories of creatures that are half human and half animal (such as sphinxes) are understandable in the same metaphorical ways. Moreover, source domains mapped onto a target domain are not unique to that domain. The source domain for conceptualizing personality, for example, is not limited to animals. It can be based on other kinds of image schemas: for example, *tactility* (*My friend is a softie*), *electricity* (*My friend is always wired*), *matter* (*My friend is a rock*), and so on. As can be seen, each source domain implies a different modeling of personality that mirrors actual personality features, which can only be truly encoded in conceptual metaphors.

These show that while the mapping mechanism itself is the same, the different source domains involve diverse image schemas that, when mapped onto the same target domain, allow for semantic nuances and involve the production of cultural connotations (Lakoff 1987; Johnson 1987; Lakoff and Johnson 1999). The schemas themselves are derivatives of physical or affective experience. For example, the experience of orientation—*up*-versus-*down*, *back*-versus-*front*, *near*-versus-*far*, and so on—leads to the formation of an image schema underlying how we conceptualize such abstractions as *happiness* (*Lately my spirits are up*), *responsibility* (*You have to face up to your problems*), among others. The common experience of containers leads to an image schema that underlies such concepts as *mind* (*My mind is full of good memories*), *emotions* (*My heart is filled with hope*), and so on. In terms of riddling, it can be seen that the mythic riddles are based on universal image schemas that are mapped onto common metaphysical concepts across the world. Subsequent forms of riddling utilize image schemas to produce situation-specific concepts, which underlie social functions such as delectation and pedagogy.

The systematicity of conceptual metaphorical thinking manifests itself via a layering of source domains, which is the source of higher-order concepts that link different source domains. For example, conceptual metaphors delivering the notion of *ideation* (how ideas, theories, and other such abstract constructs are understood) include the following source domains: *vision* (*I cannot see what you are saying*), geometry (*The ideas of Plato and Descartes are parallel in many ways*), plants (*That theory has deep roots in philosophy*), buildings (*Your theory is well constructed*), food (*That is an appetizing idea*), fashion (*His theory went out of style years ago*), and commodities (*You must package your ideas differently*). As mentioned in chapter 1, these form a network of source domains that cluster around the same target domain. Some mappings seem to cross cultural boundaries; others are culture specific. That is to say, it is likely that languages across the world commonly use source domains such as *vision* and *food* in the construction of metaphorical expressions for delivering the concept of *ideation*, but only those cultures that have traditions of Euclidean geometry and marketplace economics are likely to use source domains such as the *geometry* and *commodities* ones.

To reiterate, the source domains that underlie the early riddles are based on universally understandable image schemas. Recall the Babylonian riddle about a schoolhouse (chapter 1), which can be paraphrased as follows:

There is a house. One enters it blind and comes out seeing.

This is implanted on two image schemas: *vision* (whereby blindness is lack of knowledge) and *container* (mapped onto a schoolhouse as a container of knowledge). This type of analysis can be applied to all the mythic riddles. A sampling of early riddles taken from the sources used for this book (including Hull and Taylor 1942; Berrington and Berrington 1905; Taylor 1948, 1951; Hart 1964; Harries 1971; Alster 1976; Köngas-Maranda 1976; Fairon 1992; Ferrari 1997) resulted in the identification of the following image schemas: *paths, journeys, orientation, containers, animals, common objects* (such as *wheels*), *family members, sensory responses*, and a few others. This suggests that these riddles were among the first to utilize image schemas as the basis for abstractions such as *life, the year, knowledge, destiny*, and so on. This provides indirect, albeit substantive, support for the metaphor hypothesis. Below is a case in point of how the mapping of various source domains onto a riddle produces understanding of a particular phenomenon—the parts of a year. This is an ancient Greek riddle (Beckby 1968; paraphrased):

> A father has twice six sons. Each has thirty daughters, having one cheek white and the other black. They do not see each other's face and live only twenty-four hours.
> (*Answer: a year*)

Twelve months: *source domain* = twice six sons; each month has thirty days: *source domain* = thirty daughters apiece; each day is divided into day and night: *source domain* = each daughter has one cheek white and the other black; each day has twenty-four hours: *source domain* = each daughter lives twenty-four hours. The overall image schema is *family members*, which is mapped onto the concept of *divisions of time*.

As mentioned, after a mapping has taken place, it forms a neural blend whereby the brain has identified distinct entities in different regions through the mapping to produce a new entity in another neural region. So, in a metaphor such as *You have a long way to go*, the two distinct entities identified are *life* and *journey*. The mapping process is guided by the inference that *life is a journey*, constituting the final touch to the blend—which keeps the two entities distinct in different neural regions, while identifying them simultaneously as a single entity in a third region (see Figure 4.2).

In the case of metaphysical mappings, the region in which the topic (target) resides is an abstract concept, whereas in phenomenological mappings, it is a familiar concrete object or concept. The blending process does

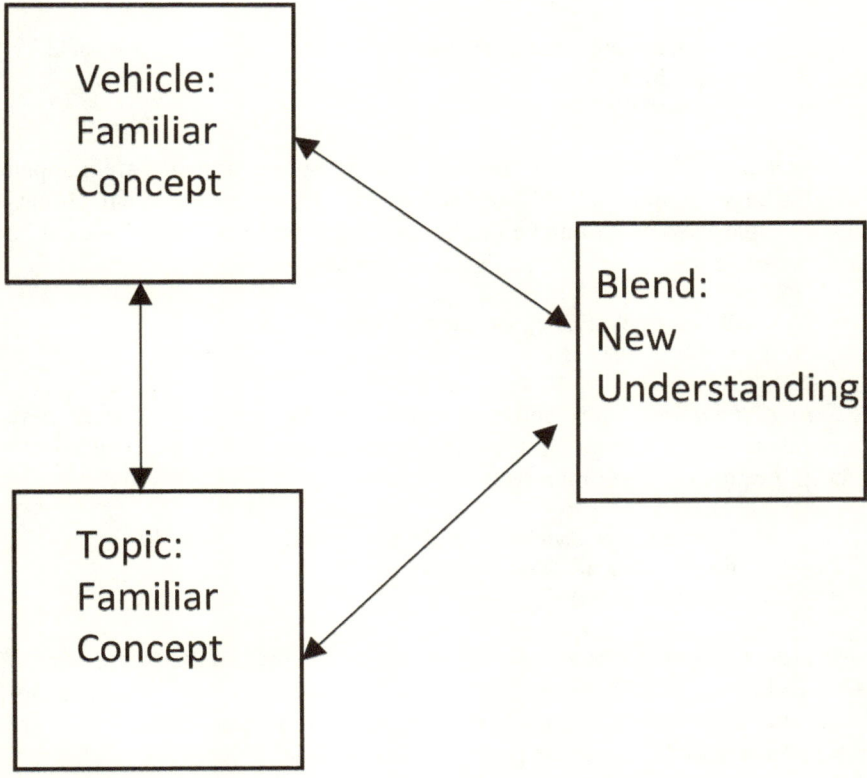

**Figure 4.2 Blending.**
*Source*: Marcel Danesi

90                                Chapter Four

not discriminate as to type of mappings; it does so according to need and situation.

As discussed (chapter 2), by late antiquity and the medieval era, phenomenological riddling emerged broadly to shed light on common everyday objects. The riddles below are cases in point from medieval Celtic riddling tradition; they are enlisted to show how the image schemas that constitute specific source domains are mapped onto everyday objects or concepts (Hull and Taylor 1942; Fairon 1992):

> What has eyes but cannot see?
> (*Answer*: a potato)

*Source domain*: eyes. The source domain is mapped onto an inanimate object via homonymy, since potato sprouts are called "eyes" metaphorically in English, resembling human eyes by their placement on the "potato head," another metaphor.

> As I went out, I met a boy with a bundle of sticks and no one could count them.
> (*Answer*: the hair)

*Source domains:* sticks and bundles. The two source domains are mapped onto the target domain of head hair because of the resemblance of hair strands to sticks that look like a bundle on the head; counting the "sticks" would be arduous since they are clustered tightly in the bundle.

> What is full of holes and can hold water?
> (*Answer*: a sponge)

*Source domains:* holes and the container. The mapping process here is motivated by a feature of sponges, which have "holes" and can absorb ("hold") water, constituting a type of container.

> From home, I made my way. On a road of roads, under them, over them, and on all sides. What are we?
> (*Answer:* rivers)

*Source domains:* paths and departure point. This is from the Norse saga of King Heidrek (Nordal and Truville-Petre 1960), as briefly mentioned in chapter 2. The mapping between roads and rivers is based on the fact that both are paths; "home" is the departure point of the river. The riddle alludes to the fact that rivers are roads that can go under, over, and on all sides of physical roads.

It is connected to the saga of King Heidrek where journeys form a constant theme, and hence the role of river journeys.

> What tears into small pieces, falling in its toothless mouth? Putting your fingers in its eyes, it will instantly prick up its ears.
> (*Answer:* scissors)

*Source domains:* parts of human anatomy. This is a medieval Persian riddle from around the ninth to eleventh century, cited in the *Kitāb al-mu'jam* (Seyed-Gohrab 2010). It sheds light on what scissors do, anthropomorphically, by mapping human anatomical parts onto the object—"toothless mouth," "eyes," and "ears."

Significantly, the exact same type of source domains and mapping strategies have been found across cultures. As Isbell and Roncalla Fernandez (1977) have observed, such riddles have been used universally as the basis for grasping the nature of things and the importance of their roles in everyday life. Below are several examples:

### *Sanskrit riddles* (Taylor 1948):

> Who moves in the air?
> (*Answer:* a bird; *source domain*: movement, which in this case occurs in "the air.")

> Who makes a noise on seeing a thief?
> *(Answer:* a dog; *source domain:* noise, which in this case is an allusion to barking.)

> Who is the enemy of lotuses?
> (*Answer:* the sun; *source domain*: sunlight, or more exactly the lack of sunlight, because although lotuses can grow in the shade, they grow best in full sunlight.)

### *African riddles* (Harries 1971; Köngas-Maranda 1976; Akínyẹmí 2015):

> I am neither inside nor outside but I am in every house.
> (*Answer*: a door; *source domain:* the container image schema, implying a *house*, into which a door is placed.)

> I have a house full of milk and crunchy food inside and the husk all over my shell.

(*Answer*: a coconut; *source domain*: the container image schema, mapped onto the coconut as a "container" of "milk and crunchy food.")

I am born tall, but I die very short. I am used inside the house.
(*Answer*: a candle; *source domains:* length and human life, which are mapped onto a candle that is "born" with its full length, but "dies very short," after its wick has been consumed.)

I have ten servants that obey to my orders, helping me whenever I need them. They nourish me, help me wear my clothes and turn the pages of my book. They never argue among themselves.
(*Answer*: fingers; *source domain*: helpers, which is actually a narrative archetype, are mapped onto the role that fingers play in helping humans get through everyday life.)

Two doors are opening and closing at the same time. But they are not doors of my house.
(*Answer*: the eyes; *source domain*: barriers, which are mapped onto eyes, given that they can open and close like doors—barriers of a specific type.)

## *Aztec riddles* (Johansson 2004):

It lives in a black forest and dies on a white stone
(*Answer:* lice on hair and fingernails; *source domains:* natural forms (forests and stones), which are mapped on the relevant parts of human anatomy with respect to lice—that is, lice are found in human head hair ("black forest") but can be eliminated with fingernails, which are as strong as stones.)

What is it always standing by the hearth curving upward?
(*Answer:* a dog's tail; *source domains:* shape and orientation, which are mapped onto the appearance of a dog's tail, as the dog is "by the hearth.")

A single red thing—it plays, talks and sings.
(*Answer:* the mouth; *source domains:* color and movements, which are mapped onto the mouth, which is "red" and which displays "movements" of specific kinds—playing, talking, and singing.)

What is it that makes colorful tortillas while flying in the air?
(*Answer:* a butterfly; *source domain:* shape, which on this case is "tortilla-like," and used to describe the movement of butterflies as they fly.)

## Chinese riddles (Rudolph 1942):

There is a small vessel filled with sauce, one vessel holding two different kinds.
(*Answer:* an egg; *source domains:* the container image schema (in this case a "vessel") and liquidity ("sauce"), which are used to describe an egg and its contents.)

Washing makes it more and more dirty; it is cleaner without washing.
(*Answer:* water; *source domains:* a particular state and its changes (cleanliness and lack thereof) are mapped onto water to describe how it changes its state as it is used for washing.)

When you use it you throw it away, and when you do not use it you bring it back.
(*Answer*: an anchor; *source domain:* movement (throwing and bringing back), which describes what is done with an anchor.)

## Philippine riddles (Hart 1964):

Not a priest, not a king but wears different kinds of clothes.
(*Answer*: a clothesline; *source domain:* arrangement (of clothes on a line), which is used in reference to the clothes worn by authoritative figures, who wear all kinds of clothes.)

Here comes Kaka, walking with an open leg.
(*Answer*: a frog; *source domain:* the sound a frog makes—"Kaka"—and how it moves—"with an open leg.")

Rice cake of the king, that you cannot divide.
(*Answer*: water; *source domains:* food and liquidity, which are used to imply that water is a luxury ("rice cake of the king"), but not a solid, which can be divided.)

This type of riddling shows how source domains came to be used as the means to cast light on everyday objects and events, rather than to explicate metaphysical notions. Some of the mappings above are metonymic or show satirical intent, which makes them situation specific. They show that irony had become a common form of discourse, constituting a type of "reverse metaphor," whereby the source domain is projected onto social ideas and events that are ridiculed via the riddle. The same evolutionary flow in riddling is seen in childhood language development, wherein irony emerges much later than metaphor, usually around pubescence. But even in metonymy and irony, the mapping mechanism is the same one—in metonymy one element (vehicle) in a domain is extracted as its source domain and then mapped against the whole domain (*an open leg* for a *frog*), in irony the source domain is selected contrastively so as to shed light, by opposition, on the target domain (*washing* makes water *dirty*).

## LAYERING

If the premise that source domain mappings constitute the conceptual backbone of language is sustainable, then a small set of such mappings should be intrinsic to the formation of the early riddles and myths. This is the core of the metaphor hypothesis. Its corollary is that as language developed diverse discourse functions, then the mappings became highly diversified and situation specific, which was the central thesis of the foregoing discussion. A related notion of the metaphor hypothesis is that the original source domains did not vanish as part of mapping strategies in later language.

An early work within conceptual metaphor theory that indirectly broaches the last point is the one by Michael Reddy (1979), who argued that root metaphors, which are based on universal image schemas, remain as conceptual mechanisms in later stages of language evolution. One of these is what he called the *conduit* schema, which is a derivative of the *container* image schema, whereby mental states (feelings, ideas, concepts, etc.) are perceived to be substances that are put into linguistic containers (words, sentences, etc.), whose meanings are then extracted by listeners or readers, akin to taking substances or objects out of their containers and then passed on to others (as if they were in a conduit). Language itself is thus a container that is used as a general conduit for conveying mental content, contained in its words and other linguistic forms. From Reddy's analysis, the notion of *frames* crystallized—defined as the various ways in which the same conceptual metaphor is framed conceptually and linguistically at all stages of language evolution, becoming intrinsic to cognition and communication (Ervas, Rossi, Ojha, and Indurkhya 2021). The following examples, which Reddy calls "core expressions," illustrate how the container image schema imbues large sections of ordinary discourse (from Reddy 1979, 285–289).

Frame 1: *thoughts are transmitted through an interpersonal conduit*
You can't get your concept across to the class that way.
His feelings came through to her only vaguely.
They never give us any idea of what they expect.

Frame 2: *thoughts are inserted into words*

Practice capturing your feelings in complete sentences.
I need to put each idea into phrases with care.
Insert that thought further down in the paragraph.

Frame 3: *words and sentences are thought containers*
The sense of loneliness is in just about every sentence.
The entire paragraph was full of emotion.
Your words are hollow—you don't mean them.

Frame 4: *thoughts are extracted from words*
I couldn't actually extract coherent ideas from that prose.
Hiding the meaning in his sentences is just his style.
They're reading things into the poem.

Frame 5: *speakers insert thoughts into the idea space*
She poured out the sorrow she'd been holding back.
He finally got those ideas out there.

Frame 6: *idea space is a container of thought*
That theory has been floating around for a century.
Those opinions are on the streets, not in a classroom.

Frame 7: *thoughts are extracted from the idea space*
I had to absorb Einstein's ideas gradually.
We couldn't get all that stuff into our brains in one afternoon.

Reddy (1979, 291–292) showed with such common examples that the notion of "thought," which is a vague one, can only be understood through such frames, which portray it as a "space" containing ideas into which people can enter to insert or take away ideas, which produces the metaphorical frames. Now, once the root conduit metaphor is imprinted in a region of the brain, it then becomes the source domain itself of all kinds of related metaphorical frames. The frames themselves can thus be labeled second-order and tertiary-order metaphors, that is, metaphors that derive from the root conduit source domain. So, an expression such as *That library has many great ideas to be discovered*, is a second-order metaphorical frame indicating that ideas are contained in words, which are on pages, which are in books, which are in libraries. As mentioned (chapter 3), this kind of derived metaphor can be explained in terms of *layering* (Danesi 2001). This implies that the source domains of the original root metaphors laid down the first layer of understanding, and that derivatives from this layer constitute second-order and third-order layers. So, a first-order layer is one that is constructed with concrete source domains—a layer whose neurological source is poetic logic (chapter 3). The conceptual metaphor in the Sphinx's Riddle, which maps phases of a *day* to phases of *life*, is a first-order metaphorical layering process, based on the universal sense that the two events are perceived as resembling each other in an imaginary way. From this root concept, other metaphorical layers can be derived—*going through life, skipping marriage is now common*, and so on.

Layering processes are explained by Lakoff (1979) as exemplifying the principle of *invariance*, namely the fact that mappings preserve the cognitive topology (image-schema structure) of the original source domain, in a way that is consistent with the inherent structure of the target domain—that is, once a *journey* is enlisted as a source domain, its features are preserved, no matter what derived frames are constructed:

> What the Invariance Principle does is guarantee that, for container schemas, interiors will be mapped onto interiors, exteriors onto exteriors, and boundaries onto boundaries; for path-schemas, sources will be mapped onto sources, goals onto goals, trajectories onto trajectories; and so on. . . . If one looks at the existing correspondences, one will see that the Invariance Principle holds: source domain interiors correspond to target domain interiors; source domain exteriors correspond to target domain exteriors; etc. As a consequence it will turn out that the image-schematic structure of the target domain cannot be violated: One cannot find cases where a source domain interior is mapped onto a target domain exterior, or where a source domain exterior is mapped onto a target domain path. This simply does not happen.

Psychologically, root conceptual metaphors are based on source domains extracted from the experience something that is familiar and easily picturable in both mental and representational terms, which are mapped onto something that cannot be experienced with the same familiarity. Once the first layer of source domains in a language has been formed, then this layer itself becomes a new productive source domain for creating evermore higher and abstract layers of concepts. Thus, for example, in utterances such as the following, the *thinking is seeing* concept is the source for more complex metaphors, that involve the blending of other source domains with the root one:

> Where did you *think up* that idea?
> I *thought over* carefully your ideas.
> You should *think out* the whole problem before attempting to solve it.

These evoke image schemas of location and movement, blended with the root image schema of *vision*. The phrase *think up* elicits a mental image of upward movement, thus portraying the abstract referent as an object being extracted physically from a kind of mental terrain; *think over* evokes the image of scanning with the mind's eye; and *think out* elicits an image of extracting something so that it can be held up to the scrutiny of the mind's eye. These frames allow users to locate and identify abstract ideas in relation to spatiotemporal contexts, although such contexts are purely imaginary. It is as if these imaginary movements allow us to locate thoughts in the mind. Overall, they manifest the formation of a second-order metaphor that can be formulated as *thinking is visual scanning*.

The third-order layer of metaphorical reasoning is a level made up of further derived metaphorical frames that assume culture-specific symbolic forms. For example, *illumination* or *enlightenment* is a third-order metaphorical frame, extending the *thinking is seeing* primary layer into the domain of culture, as can be seen in metaphors of knowledge involving light and even eras of history designated as *dark ages* or *the Enlightenment*. The higher the density of layering, the more abstract and, thus, more culture specific, the concept (see Figure 4.3).

In a relevant work, Pepicello and Green (1984, 128) indirectly support both framing and layering theory, claiming that "riddles are metalinguistic, i.e., they are a way of using language to deal with language." However, the two authors take a different slant on the role of metaphor in riddles, which is more in line with early transformational grammar than with conceptual metaphor theory (Chomsky 1957, 1965). But their main thesis is a relevant one. They portray first-order riddling as "licensed confusion" that involves an admixture of phonological, morphological, and syntactic levels of linguistic structure. These are conceived and delivered orally, eventually being written down. The relevant aspect of their work is that riddles oscillate between grammatical and metaphorical ambiguity and that their framing in terms of a question-and-answer dialectic suggests that riddles may actually be the source of dialogue—which is fascinating and relevant in itself.

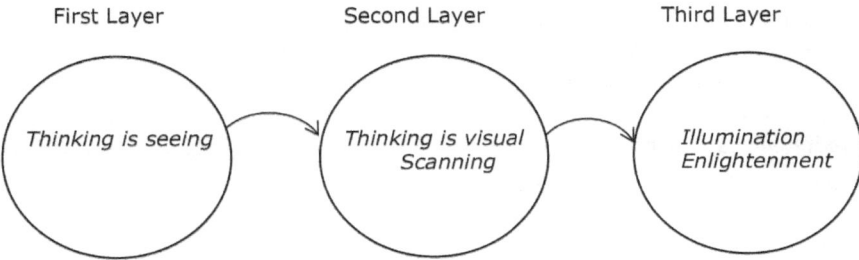

**Figure 4.3 Layering.**
*Source*: Marcel Danesi

Given the root conceptual function of ancient riddles, it comes as little surprise to find that they were used in the early civilizations to educate children so as to impart literacy and reasoning to them in a playful way (above and chapter 2). The riddle found inscribed on a clay tablet dating back to Babylonian-Sumerian times around 2000 BCE has been discussed several times as an example of how ancient societies viewed the importance of riddles (Taylor 1948). It is one of twenty-five riddles found etched on a clay tablet that were translated in 1960 by Edmund Gordon. Given its relevance to the metaphor hypothesis, it is worthwhile revisiting here, since it is grounded on several root image schemas—*conduit, animal, container*, and *vision* ones (Alster 1976):

> A house, covered with a veil like a secret box is based on a foundation like the skies, and set on a base like a goose. One enters it blind and leaves seeing.
> (*Answer:* a schoolhouse)

The image of the *skies* implies that the heavens (the gods) are the conduits of all knowledge, which is also found in many ancient myths that portray knowledge as descending from above, such as the myth of Prometheus, who brought knowledge down to humans from the heavens. A *goose* is known for its protection of its nest, and thus, by extension, as a metaphor for preserving the knowledge that was given birth inside the schoolhouse. The image of a *secret box* is based on the *container* image schema, implying that knowledge remains hidden or secret until it is taken out of the box (Danesi 2018). Finally, entering *blind* into the schoolhouse—a container of knowledge—allows us to *see* what is in the secret box after completing our education.

Another root metaphor that is found in riddles and myths alike is that of *knowledge* as growing on *trees*, which emerges at around the same time as the conduit metaphor (Berrington and Berrington 1905). The *tree of knowledge* root metaphor with knowledge growing like "branches" and "roots," has remained a source of subsequent layering—*Psychology traces its roots to ancient philosophy*, *Those ideas have led to branches of knowledge*, and so on. Another common first-order strategy is personification, which produces anthropomorphic metaphors, whereby an inanimate object or event is ascribed human qualities, as the following riddles from antiquity and the medieval era illustrate (Berrington and Berrington 1905; Hickman du Bois 1912; Taylor 1951; Keyne and Amsel 2014):

> I view the world in little space, always changing place. I do not eat, but procure what millions do devour.
> (*Answer:* the sun)

There's not a kingdom on the earth, that I have travelled over and
over, through towns fields and meadows green, day or night, but I
neither am nor can be seen.
(*Answer:* the wind)

Through all my days, I've been trampled under feet. When I decay,
the person who made me cannot save my sole.
(*Answer:* a shoe)

Four wings I have, yet I never fly; and though my body often moves
around, upon the self-same spot I'm always found. I chew for man
before he can be fed.
(*Answer:* a windmill)

Though it be cold, I wear no clothes. The frost and snow I never
fear, and yet I wander far and near. My diet is forever good. What
Providence doth send for food, I neither buy, nor sell, nor lack.
(*Answer:* a fish)

I fly to any foreign parts, assisted by my spreading wings. My body
holds a hundred hearts. I issue fire from my side.
(*Answer:* a ship).

Layering can be seen, in some instances, in how source domains are blended to produce a complex riddle (as in some of the riddles discussed above). Consider the riddles below (from Taylor 1951):

They come out at night without being fetched; by day they disappear without being stolen.
(*Answer*: the stars)

*Blended source domains*: time (night) and natural event structure (stars are events that are beyond human intervention).

It never was, but always will be. No one has ever seen me, nor
ever will.
(*Answer*: tomorrow)

*Blended source domains*: personification and event structure (how days follow each other and are named accordingly).

It murmurs but does not talk; it has a bed but it does not sleep; it has
a mouth but does not eat.
(*Answer*: a river)

*Blended source domains*: personification and movement to describe rivers.

> No sooner spoken than it is broken.
> (*Answer*: silence).

*Blended source domains*: voice and objects, which are blended to describe silence.

> If the sun sets, it will let you see a flower-garden; but if you look at it after dawn, you will see an empty garden.
> (*Answer*: the sky)

*Blended source domains*: gardens and the sky, used to describe visibility in the light.

Higher-order layering is the source for situation-specific metaphors, such as the ones discussed above. Take, for example, the source domain of Euclidean geometry. In Western culture the various ideas and concepts connected with this type of geometry have become habits of mind, because of the simple fact that it has been taught to children in school since the beginning of obligatory education. Overall, geometric metaphors can be seen to be based on a *geometry is spatial vision* image schema—which is itself a framing of the *thinking is seeing* metaphor. The linguistic metaphors that the blending produces are culture specific—that is, they are understood by cultures that assign the same value to Euclidean geometry:

> Don't you think those ideas are rather *circular*?
> I don't see the *point* you are making.
> Her ideas are *central* to the discussion.
> Their ideas are *diametrically* opposite.
> Those ideas are *parallel* in many ways.
> My idea is in *line* with yours.

A source domain that can be ascribed to the deepest layer of cognition is that of the *journey*, which is mapped onto experiences that relate to all facets of life (Ferrari 1997; Katz 2008). The Sphinx's Riddle too is grounded on the journey metaphor, given that Oedipus went on a journey to Thebes to search for the truth of his own existence, matching his three phrases of life—infancy (when the prophecy was uttered), adulthood (when he embarked on the journey of self-discovery), and old age (when he finally had to come to grips with his destiny). As Kövecses (2002, 9) has cogently argued and amply illustrated, the *life is a journey* metaphor imbues all kinds of concepts at different layered levels (or blends):

Humans are journeyers.
The life span is a journey event.
Life's goal is the journey's destination.
Short-term goals are journey stops.
Lifestyle is the manner of the journey.
Life companion is the journey companion.

As discussed in this chapter, many root source domains are based on the human body, which is mapped onto all kinds of things and phenomena. This shows that anthropomorphism is a fundamental source of understanding. Below are some examples (Danesi 2020):

What becomes pregnant without conceiving and fat without eating?
(*Answer:* a cloud)

This is an ancient Babylonian riddle, mentioned briefly in chapter 1. The rain inflates and expands a cloud, appearing pregnant.

Four hang, four sprang, two point the way, two to ward off dogs,
one dangles after, always rather dirty. What am I?.
(*Answer:* a cow)

This is the complete version of an ancient Norse riddle, mentioned previously, describing the anatomy of a cow and what its organs allow the cow to do, such as chasing away dogs—it too is based on a personification of an animal, portraying it as possessing language, and thus able to ask human questions ("What am I?")

This woman has not been to the riverside for water, but there is water in her tank
(*Answer:* a coconut).

This riddle comes from the Kwa language of Ewe culture, a culture that covers areas of Ghana, Togo, and Benin. The likely reason why the coconut is compared to a woman is that it is a "bearer"—a coconut bears water in a way that resembles how a woman bears children, who survive in water (amniotic fluid) in the womb.

In discussing layering the term *analogy* is inevitably subsumed. Traditionally, analogy implies an intentional comparison between two things (or domains), typically for the purpose of explanation or clarification. Research in conceptual metaphor theory has suggested that analogies show the same kind of mapping structure of metaphor—only their functions differ. Dedre Gentner (1983) who was among the first to characterize analogy as a type of structure mapping, thus aligning the notion with conceptual metaphor theory. Subsequent work (Holyoak and Thagard 1995; Hummel and Holyoak 2005; Doumas, Hummel, and Sandhofer 2008) has further aligned conceptual metaphors with analogies.

## EVENT STRUCTURE AND INVARIANCE

A major claim of conceptual metaphor theory (Lakoff 1979, 1987; Lakoff and Johnson 1999) is that *event structure* mappings are primary or root processes, involving target domains such as *states, change, process, actions, causes, purposes,* and *means,* which are linked to domains involving such concepts as *space, motion,* and *force.* If this claim is valid, then it should show up in ancient riddling artifacts. As a test case, it can be assessed by examining the Riddle of the Sphinx and the myth in which it is embedded (the Oedipus story) for event structure. If it fits the riddle, then the same type of analysis could be extended to other mythic riddles.

Event structure has various components, which are found as such in the riddle and the Oedipus myth as follows:

States are locations, perceived as bounded regions.

Morning, noon, and evening in the riddle are states that are conceived as locations in time and thus as temporally bounded regions.

Changes are movements, in and out of the bounded regions.

Moving from morning to noon to evening unfolds in terms of moving from one bounded region of time to another.

Causes are forces.

Oedipus's fate is perceived as a force of destiny.

Actions are self-propelled movements.

Oedipus's journey to self-discovery is self-propelled.

Purposes are destinations.

The goal of determining who he is impels Oedipus to travel to Thebes—the destination.

Means are paths to destinations.

In order to achieve his goal of self-discovery, Oedipus embarks on a path to a specific destination (Thebes).

Difficulties are impediments to motion.

Oedipus encounters a challenger on his way to Thebes, who becomes an impediment to his journey.

Progress is a travel schedule.

The schedule in Oedipus's case is his search for understanding. The riddle enfolds the travel path as a *phase* metaphor.

External events are moving objects.

While in Thebes, Oedipus eventually discovers that the plague that has beset the city is moving around him, whereby he discovers its source.

Long term, purposeful activities are journeys.

The overall theme of the Oedipus story is that journeys are purposeful, even if they end up tragically.

As Lakoff (1979) puts it, event structure involves the blending of states "whose parts interact in complex ways," which involves specific types of entailments (Lakoff 1979), which are also embedded in the Oedipus myth:

Manner of action is manner of motion.

Oedipus takes the action of going on a journey to discover who he is; so the journey itself is the manner of motion.

Aids to action are aids to motion.

Oedipus asserts that nothing can get in his way to get to the truth. His aid is the oracular prophecy pronounced at his birth.

A different means of achieving a result is a different path.

We know that Oedipus should have sought a different path to gain self-knowledge. In effect, he should have taken a *different path*, to avoid disaster, but he did not.

Careful action is careful motion.

We know that Oedipus is walking a fine line between self-knowledge and destiny.

Purposeful action is self-propelled motion to a destination.

Oedipus himself decided to take the journey to Thebes.

Starting an action is starting out on a path.

Oedipus's action to avoid the oracular prophecy is to start out on a specific path—a journey to Thebes. The tragic irony is that the path, like the phases of a day, is predetermined.

Success is reaching the end of the path.

Oedipus does indeed reach his goal successfully at the end of his path to Thebes, after solving the Sphinx's Riddle, even though the result is not what he had anticipated.

The corollary to event structure is called the *inheritance hierarchies* supposition—which states that metaphorical mappings do not occur autonomously from one another, but organized in hierarchical structures. This is clearly isomorphic to layering theory above, and thus needs little commentary here. What is relevant is that the inheritance processes account for a range of mappings, including personification, proverbialization, and analogy (Lakoff 1979).

## Personification

Mapping processes that involve personification, such as personifying death as a chess player playing the grim reaper (as in Ingmar Bergman's 1957 film, *The Seventh Seal*). Events (like death) are understood in terms of actions by some agent (like reaping). As Lakoff points out, it is the agent that is typically personified. This explains concepts such as the notion that death is a departure event (from life). So, "if we understand this event as an action on the part of some causal agent—someone who brings about, or helps to bring about, departure—then we can account for figures like drivers, coachmen, footmen, etc." (Lakoff 1979). There is also a causal aspect to death: the passage of time will eventually result in death, like the end of the day (Riddle of the Sphinx).

## Proverbialization

Proverbs are metaphorical mappings, based on shaping poetic wisdom via metaphor (chapter 3). The early riddles were essentially proverbs, displaying a similar type of event structure. For instance, the English proverb of *Too many irons in the fire*, which describes someone attempting to perform too many things at once so that none of them are done well, shows the causal structure of events and their structure-preserving nature—once irons are put into the fire, the fire causes them to become too hot.

## Analogy

As Lakoff and Turner (1989) have amply illustrated in their work, the *generic is specific* metaphor is used to produce understanding, and it is at the basis of analogy. In the Riddle of the Sphinx, the *phases* metaphor is essentially a manifestation of the notion that the *generic* [life] *is specific* [daytime].

## REFINING THE METAPHOR HYPOTHESIS

The metaphor hypothesis has been adopted in this book to claim that metaphorical cognition is at the core of language, as separate from (but related to) primordial nominative speech, and that it crystallized in the early riddles and myths. A central aspect of the hypothesis is that metaphor is the product of a poetic logic—a way of connecting things via resemblance and inference. Conceptual metaphor theory allows for a refinement of this hypothesis by providing a framework for assessing the structure of metaphorical cognition in terms of event structure, invariance, framing, and so on.

The early riddles are based on root metaphors—journeys, containers, conduits, and so on—which are embedded contemporaneously in the early myths. The myth of Pandora's *box,* for example, is based on the container schema. It recounts how Prometheus gave humanity the gift of fire, the symbol of intelligence (the conduit image schema), which he stole from Mount Olympus in a fennel stalk, against the wishes of Zeus, who did not want humans to become intelligent. To punish humanity for Prometheus's crime, Zeus ordered the gods to make a creature to both delight and torment them— Pandora. She was given a box with instructions not to open it. But curiosity got the better of her, so she opened the box and out poured all the illnesses and griefs of the world. Only hope remained inside.

Analyzing riddles and early myths from the conceptual metaphor perspective reveals two main things: (1) that they are based on root image schemas—conduits, journeys, phases, containers, plants, animals, and so on; (2) that the same schemas are mapped on the same types of ontological target domains (*life*, *destiny*, *knowledge*, and so on); and (3) that the image schemas entail each other and are often blended together. For instance, the *vision* source domain is often blended with the *container* one as exemplified by the Babylonian schoolhouse riddle (above); the *journey* and the *phases* image schemas are blended in many riddles, including the Riddle of the Sphinx; and so on. In effect, riddles document what is perhaps the first appearance of the use of language to *think* in complex ways and to enter into a dialogue with others in sophisticated, meaningful ways through framing and layering—a fact that has remained basic to discourse to this day. So, for instance, when the topic of *ideas* comes up in a conversation, speakers of English tend to deliver it by navigating conceptually through the various source domains that cluster around it according to need, whim, or situation. For example, the sentence *I can't see why your ideas are not catching on, given that they have deep roots and lie on solid ground* has been guided by the blending of three source domains (*vision*, *plants*, and *buildings*).

Not all abstract thought manifests a clustering blended structure. There is another form of associative metaphorical structure that manifests itself commonly in everyday discourse, whereby different target domains are delivered by identical source domains. This process can be called *radiation*, since it can be envisioned as a single source domain "radiating outwards" to map different target domains (Danesi 2007). For example, the *plant* source domain not only allows us to conceptualize ideas (*That idea has deep ramifications*), but also such other abstract concepts as *love* (*Our love has deep roots*), *influence* (*His influence is sprouting all over*), *success* (*Her career has borne great fruit*), *knowledge* (*That discipline has many branches*), *wisdom* (*His wisdom has deep roots*), and *friendship* (*Their friendship is starting to bud just now*), among others.

Radiation can be defined as the tendency to envisage some abstract concepts as implicating each other through a specific metaphorical network of source domains. It might explain why we talk of seemingly different things, such as *wisdom* and *friendship*, with the same metaphorical images. Clustering, on the other hand, explains why we use different metaphorical vehicles to deliver the same concept. It allows people to connect source domains as they talk.

## EPILOGUE

Riddles originate at the same time as the earliest myths. They emerge, therefore, in the age of the gods (as Vico called the era, chapter 3). The myths are themselves riddles, posing questions about the mystery of existence and attempting to come to grips with the human condition. However, not all the ancient riddles were devised to test the acumen of mythic heroes or as self-fulfilling prophecies. As mentioned in chapter 2, they subserved ludic, literary, pedagogical, and other social functions, already in antiquity (albeit a later antiquity). The core objective of all riddles is *understanding* in terms of connections and associations of various kinds. Starting with nominative speech, which accompanied gesture, and progressing to language via metaphor, humans have evolved beyond simple nomination to conceptualization. Vico explained this evolutionary thrust in his own way as follows, long before conceptual metaphor theory (Bergin and Fisch 1984, 18): "a mute language of signs and physical objects having natural relations to the ideas they wished to express" [referred to as *nominative speech* in this book] . . . "that spoken by means of heroic emblems, or similitudes, comparisons, images, metaphors, and natural descriptions" [referred to as gap-filling *phenomenological* metaphorical language in this book] . . . and "human language using words agreed upon by the people" [subsequent *layering* of image schemas to produce full-blown language].

Human culture is impossible to explain satisfactorily. The term often used to refer to the cultural sphere in human life is the *semiosphere* (Lotman 1991), which at the very least characterizes it as a sphere containing human-made signs and symbols, as opposed to the *biosphere*, as containing signs and forms produced by nature. British anthropologist Edward B. Tylor defined culture in his 1871 book *Primitive Culture* as "a complex whole including knowledge, belief, art, morals, law, custom, and any other capability or habit acquired by human beings as members of society." Tylor's definition was also one of the first to differentiate qualitatively between *culture* and *society*. Although these terms continue to be used commonly as synonyms in many languages, in actual fact they refer to different things. Within a social collectivity, there can, and frequently does, exist more than one culture. In an opposite manner, several societies can be thought of as belonging to the same general culture. Societies are simultaneously the geographical and historical "reifications" (manifestations) of cultures. The origins of culture as a semiospheric system begins with the first myths and riddles. In line with Jaynes's (1976) bicameral mind hypothesis, it can be claimed, that when the two chambers became specialized in processing mental functions, they allowed language to come into existence, forming the basis of human culture—a basis that displays primary metaphorical structures. So, in neural terms, the initial stages of language involve the poetic, creative right hemisphere, which is the locus of metaphor, after which the left hemisphere enters the process to give formal stability to the thoughts generated in in the metaphorical right hemisphere. From this springs conceptual language, which in turn subserves discourse functions.

As Lakoff (1979) aptly put it, "metaphor is a major and indispensable part of our ordinary, conventional way of conceptualizing the world, and that our everyday behavior reflects our metaphorical understanding of experience." In this framework, literal meaning is a residue of the nominative function of early speech. As Lakoff (1979) insightfully asserts, "a sentence like *The balloon went up* is not metaphorical, nor is the old philosopher's favorite *The cat is on the mat*. But as soon as one gets away from concrete physical experience and starts talking about abstractions or emotions, metaphorical understanding is the norm."

*Chapter Five*

# Language Origins

**PROLOGUE**

Throughout this book, the notion of *speech* has been constrained to imply the use of nominative signs that function much like the various identifier signals of other species but develop referential complexity as they are used; the term *language* has been used instead in reference to the use of verbal signs to understand abstract, complex referents or else to name things that are unknown or have been left unnamed. This is, of course, an artificial dichotomy, since nominative speech and conceptual language often intersect ontologically. Nonetheless, there is evidence that the two emerge in an evolutionary sequence. Derek Bickerton (2014), for instance, has claimed that speech is a displacement of animal communication—an advanced exaptation that is not bound by the stimulus-response constraints to which the latter is tied. Language, on the other hand, displaces the referential response system, becoming the source for *thinking* about the world, not just *referring* to it.

This chapter will tie the thematic threads of previous chapters together so as to summarize the metaphor hypothesis. In the phylogenetic scenario being elaborated here, speech involves naming concrete referents such as giving names to "mother," "father," "sun," "stars," "snake," and so on. Whatever underlying phonetic mechanisms are involved, the function of such speech is nomination (discussed further below). Nomination can also involve metaphor, as, for instance, naming the bottom part of a mountain as a *foot*, the leading figure in a family or kinship system as the *head*, and so on. Full-blown *language* emerges when metaphor subserves the formation of complex thoughts via mappings, such as *life as a journey, knowledge occurs in containers*, and so on (see Table 5.1).

The philological fact that mythic riddles coincide with the founding myths of a culture, supports the premise that language is born as *mythos* and thus

**Table 5.1 Speech and Language**

| Type | Function | Examples |
|---|---|---|
| Nominative speech | Concrete names for common everyday referents | Words for "mother," "father," "sun," etc. |
| Metaphorical speech | Naming referents via metaphor | Words for "foot" or "head" in reference to the bottom part of a mountain or the main figure in a family, respectively |
| Language | Complex thoughts (abstractions, generalizations, etc.) | *Life as a journey, as phases of a day, as a path,* and so on |

is a product of poetic logic. This is why the conceptual metaphors that are found in the ancient mythic riddles are based on virtually identical source domains. This is in line with Émile Durkheim's (1912) notion that myths arose as responses to existence, binding people ontologically and thus culturally. Bronislaw Malinowski (1923) claimed that myth was not merely a story, but an unconscious language that allows a group to give their experiences a sense of conceptual-cultural unity. The early riddles have been used in this book as evidence of the appearance of this unity of mind. Each ancient riddle was a metaphorical interpretation of some phenomenon, event, or action, not just a labeling or retelling of it. As time progressed, riddles took on different discursive qualities, subserving various social functions, thus mirroring the evolution of discourse functions.

## FROM SPEECH TO LANGUAGE

A qualitative distinction between language and speech was formulated for the first time by Ferdinand de Saussure (1916), who saw language (*langue*) as a faculty of mind and speech (*parole*) as the ability to communicate via this faculty. While he is often critiqued for making this distinction artificially, viewing *langue* as a system of arbitrary signs unaffected by its use in communication, he nonetheless realized that physical speech, as the phonic means for making word signs, was the basis of language as a thought system (Saussure 1916, 112):

> The characteristic role of language with respect to thought is not to create a material phonic means for expressing ideas but to serve as a link between thought and sound, under conditions that of necessity bring about the reciprocal delimitations of units. Thought, chaotic by nature, has to become ordered in the process of its decomposition. Neither are thoughts given material form nor are sounds transformed into mental entities; the somewhat mysterious fact is rather

that "thought-sound" implies division, and that language works out its units while taking shape between two shapeless masses. Visualize the air in contact with a sheet of water; if the atmospheric pressure changes, the surface of the water will be broken up into a series of divisions, waves; the waves resemble the union or coupling of thought with phonic substance.

The term *speech* as used commonly today is roughly equivalent to Saussure's *parole*. As such, it refers to both the physiological capacity to articulate sounds (or by extension to write words) and the ability to use *langue* for communicative and other expressive purposes. In this book the term has been used only in a phylogenetic sense as the use of the vocal apparatus to name things concretely; whereas *language* is understood as the capacity to form thoughts by using words in some complex way, such as in combination to form phrases and larger forms. The term *phenomenological* metaphor has been used in this book in reference to how things are named via metaphor—a function that emerges in tandem with language as a conceptual system. The distinction between speech and language as adopted here is a highly restrictive one, since these are interactive components in the evolution of language as a fully developed thought system. It is a convenient one, however, for tracing a flow from nomination to conceptualization. The origin of speech is thus the starting point for considering the metaphor hypothesis.

As discussed in chapter 1, of all the positions put forth to explain the origins of speech, *echoic* theory remains a widely accepted one to this day. It states that the first words were forged as iconic signs imitating naturally occurring sounds (Stam 1976; Bickerton 2014). The reconstruction of proto-words (also discussed in chapter 1) provides strong evidence in favor of this theory, since they commonly reveal the tendency of the first words to be imitative constructs of sounds in the environment. It also has shown that the early speech forms were intended to encode common referents—family members, parts of the body, objects found in nature, and so on. Included in this hypothetical scenario are the effortful grunts that may also have become words during various laborious activities, as Stross (1976, 22) explains:

> Groups of early humans, straining with the intense and common effort necessary to move a fallen log or other such occupation, came to emit spontaneous grunts which were partly consonantal and which would eventually be used to signal common exertion in much the same way that today we use "heave" or "pull" in group lifting or pulling efforts. Eventually the grunts used for coordinating the efforts of many persons in a rhythmic way came to be associated with the work performed and then to stand for the work itself in symbolic communication.

In effect, the first forms of speech were likely devised to name anything that occurred regularly in the immediate environment and perceived as necessary to everyday life. This included human reactions to events, such as refutation or denial which took on a specific articulatory form via nasal phonemes. As Swadesh (1971, 193) explains, this may be the source of words for negation:

> The use of nasal phonemes in the negative in so many languages of the world must in some way be related to the prevailing nasal character of the grunt. In English, the vocable of denial is almost always nasal; but it can vary from a nasalized vowel to any of the nasal consonants: ã!ã, õ!õ, m!m, n!n. . . . Why is nasality so common? Surely because it results from the relaxation of the velum; the most usual position of the velum is down, and the most relaxed form of grunt is nasal. The prevalence of nasals in the negative . . . may therefore be due to the fact that they are based on grunts.

Alongside vocal speech forms, there is strong evidence that gesture emerged at the same time to complement or even precede the vocal nominative function (referring to things in the world via locations and movements; Hewes 1973, 1976). As Stross (1976, 22) argues, gesture certainly must have played a key role in displacing reference from the immediacy of its referents:

> It is easy to imagine bipedal animals gesturing to attract attention or pointing out a particular object with a wave of the hand. Perhaps you can even visualize a group of prelinguistic humans imitating the shapes of things with hand gestures or pointing to parts of the body. Association of the gesture with the thing indicated would then have to be extended to situations in which the object was not present.

The transition from gesture to vocal speech has always been a difficult one to explain. As discussed (chapter 1), Richard Paget (1930) suggested that the transition occurred via osmosis, whereby the gestural movements were unconsciously imitated by lip and tongue movements, replacing the former unconsciously. Speculative explanatory frameworks such as echoism and gesture theory are based on inferences as to what the first words were like and what sounds (or manual forms) subserved their formation. In 1959, Arthur Diamond argued that speech became language when the nomination process shifted to common bodily actions like breaking, killing, cutting, and so on to produce the first verbs. As these were added to existing nouns—names for objects and creatures—full language emerged. But this does not explain how such complex speech forms were combined to produce complex thoughts. Moreover, it does not explain how echoic forms eventually evolved metaphorical structure for naming things unknown and for constructing complex thoughts. Nor does it explain the connection between metaphor and grammar (as discussed in chapter 3).

Research on the origins question has produced a fairly good picture of how vocal speech itself came about—a picture that is worthwhile revisiting here in a nutshell because it is suggestive of how metaphor could have eventually evolved from it—a hypothesis that was actually put forth by Rousseau, as discussed in chapter 1, but rarely followed up by language scientists. The plaster casts of skulls found at archeological sites, used to reconstruct hominid brains, have revealed that both Neanderthal and Cro-Magnon humans (pre-30,000 BCE) had brains of similar size to contemporary humans as well as structurally similar vocal tracts (Lieberman 1972). A second major finding is that vocal speech was developed at the expense of an anatomical system intended primarily for breathing and eating. As Laitman (1983, 1990) has argued, the fact that the position of the larynx in human infants is high in the neck, like it is in that of other primates, provides indirect evidence of the ontogeny repeats phylogeny theory, as used to hypothesize the origins scenario retroactively. At an early point in the first year of life, the larynx descends into the neck (Krantz 1988). The descent is a phenomenon that is unique to humans, producing a pharyngeal chamber above the vocal cords that can modify sound. By examining fossil skulls, Laitman (1983) found that the australopithecines of southern and eastern Africa of 1.5 to 4 million years ago had the skull-larynx configuration of apes and human infants, with the larynx high in the vocal tract. Those hominids, therefore, could not have had speech, although they may have had gesture. Laitman documented the same skull-larynx pattern in *Homo erectus* (1.5 million to 300,000 or 400,000 years ago). It was not until the arrival of *Homo sapiens* that he found evidence for the formation of a lowered vocal tract that had the capacity to produce articulate speech.

The lowering of the larynx gives the child the ability to articulate verbal sounds and, gradually, to form words and other early verbal structures. The same lowering allowed early humans to create speech. Now, the question of why the lowering occurred in the first place is explained as a consequence of bipedalism. In standing up straight, the early humans developed an upright posture that was conducive to the larynx lowering under the force of gravity. According to Lieberman (1972, 1984) this started 100,000 years ago. Using endocranial casting—the method of reconstructing the brain in a skull by comparing the characteristics of the skull to what is known about brain anatomy—Lieberman found that in reconstructed adult skulls (endocasts) that are older than 100,000 years the anatomical and neural characteristics for speech are lacking. They are present however in those that are less than 100,000 years old. Lieberman thus concluded that a fully developed capacity for articulate speech was in place 100,000 years ago, not before. The descent in infants is explained as an inheritance feature of contemporary humans from their biological past.

To reiterate here, the evidence coming out of the reconstruction of proto-languages (chapter 1) indicates that the nominative process was based on iconicity (Fitch 2012; Bickerton 2014; Hurford 2014; Everett 2019)—a key semiotic notion as elaborated by Charles Peirce (1931). Now, the question becomes: How did speech become language? In terms of the metaphor hypothesis the claim is that it did so, in a nutshell, via the emergence of metaphor on the evolutionary timetable, around the time of the early civilizations, and this implies that metaphor is itself a derivative of iconicity—a manner of seeking resemblances not only in phonic substance, but also in ontological substance. So, the transition from speech to language was an iconic process, whereby the speech forms were used to discover or perhaps even establish similarities among abstractions. In this scenario, let us assume that at some advanced point in time some human decided to name an abstract concept *love*, on the basis of a feeling the individual shared with others in the community. At that point, a need may have arisen to understand this feeling in more concrete terms (that is, iconically)—hence mapping the feeling against various experiences, such as the experience of paths or journeys, which resemble the development of love in an imaginary sense. This leads to metaphors of love based on this kind of abstract iconicity—*Their love is on the right path*, *They are on their way to marriage*, and so on.

Now, while this scenario is highly speculative and anecdotal, indirect evidence comes from childhood development—again under the rubric of ontogeny repeating phylogeny. If a young child were to ask an adult "What is love?," the adult would not contemplate giving the child a dictionary-style definition of love, such as "an affective response to some affectionate signal emitted by another human being." What the person is more likely to do is to relate the experience of love to something that is familiar to the child: "Well, you know, love is the feeling you get when your mommy or daddy kisses you." Or else the person might tell or read the child a story that illustrates what love is all about. In this anecdotal scenario the origins of metaphor as an iconic strategy can be discerned. As the metaphor hypothesis implies, a similar scenario could have easily occurred in the transition from speech to language, which made its appearance in the first riddles and myths.

Insights into the transition are provided as well by the theory of sound symbolism, which claims that words and various structures are formed via the imprinting of the sounds made by referents into the phonemic make-up of the words coined for the referents. Sound symbolism is a specific form of verbal iconicity, based on the resemblance between sounds and meanings (Hinton, Nichols, and Ohala 1994).

Many ancient writers actually linked sound, writing characters, and meaning speculatively. For instance, in ancient Chinese society, as Schuessler (2007) points out, words with /m/ were associated with something black, those made with /n/ were linked instead to something soft or flexible, and those with /k/ with some abrupt action. In Plato's *Cratylus* (Plato 2013), Socrates is portrayed as suggesting that words were originally constructed with sounds that reflected some property of their referents. However, the many counterexamples given to Socrates by his interlocutor, Hermogenes, leads the philosopher to admit that his view was, after all, just speculative. In the seventeenth century, John Locke (1690) dismissed such speculation outright, pointing out that if sound symbolism was a principle of language then we would all be speaking the same language. He maintained that the relation between words and their phonetic structure is arbitrary, with only a few onomatopoeic exceptions, as did Saussure (1916) later in the nineteenth century.

The scientific investigation of sound symbolism as providing clues to the origin of speech started in the 1920s (Jespersen 1922). In the 1950s, Morris Swadesh (1951, 1959, 1971) championed it as a major principle of language design, drawing attention to the fact that it is an operative principle in the formation of words and even grammatical categories across languages. For instance, he argued that front vowels (/i/-type and /e/-type vowels) are used commonly to construct words in which "nearness" was implied, in contrast to back vowels (/a/-type, /o/-type, and /u/-type vowels), which are used instead to construct words in which the opposite concept of "distance" was implied—in English common examples are *here* versus *there*, *near* versus *far*, and *this* versus *that*. In a relevant study, Brown, Black, and Horowitz (1955) discussed several experiments that seemed to substantiate Swadesh's claims. For instance, in one experiment, speakers of English listened to pairs of antonyms from a language unrelated to English and then were asked to guess, given the English equivalents, which English word translated which foreign word. For instance, when asked to match the Chinese words *ching* and *chung* to English *light* and *heavy*, not necessarily in that order, it was found that most English speakers matched *ching* to *light* and *chung* to *heavy*, which matches the general connotations of the Chinese words. A little later, Brown (1958) expanded sound symbolism theory, giving the example of Samoan *ongololo* referring to "centipede" as an example of how the syllables in a word correspond to the number of distinct elements in the sound, object, or action perceived in the referent. The same process is extended to shapes. In Chinese, visual contour leads to the sound symbolic modeling of the feelings that the shapes evoke.

Benjamin Lee Whorf also saw the interconnection between phonemes and meanings as an intrinsic one, suggesting that it guides our interpretation of words and thus of reality. He put it as follows (Whorf 1956, 267–268):

> In the psychological experiments, human subjects seem to associate the experiences of bright, cold, sharp, hard, high, light (in weight), quick, high-pitched, narrow, and so on in a long series, with each other; and conversely, the

experiences of dark, warm, yielding, soft, blunt, low, heavy, slow, low-pitched, wide, etc. in another long series. This occurs whether the words for such associated experiences resemble them or not, but the ordinary person is likely to perceive a relation to words only when it is a relation of likenesses to such a series in the vowels and consonants of words.

It was Margaret Magnus (1999) who amassed a significant corpus of data to show that words that utilize the same phoneme categories tend to coalesce around a similar core of meanings and that different phonemes suggest different clusters of reference. The relation is not one to one—that is, one cannot predict what phoneme a given language will use for imprinting some audio-aural property of a particular referent into the formation of its words, but the relation itself is always implied. Magnus put forth the following four basic sound-symbolic processes:

1. *Onomatopoeia* involves a straightforward, intentional imitation of sound properties: *splash, pop, bang*.
2. *Clustering* refers to words that share a phoneme tend to cluster around a referential domain; so, if /h/ is used for *house*, then a disproportionate amount of words will start with /h/ within the same lexical field: *hut, home, hovel, habitat*.
3. *Iconism* refers to words that have similar or analogous referents. For instance, words such as *stomp, tramp,* and *step* show the phonemic pattern of /m/ + /p/ or /s/ + /t/, sharing semantic linkages.
4. *Phenomimes* and *psychomimes* are "quasi onomatopoeic" words; the former evoke latent sound reference and the latter psychological states. The word *duck* is a phenomine because it suggests the sound made by a "duck," already encoded onomatopoeically with *quack*. *Ugh* is a psychomime that is meant to represent some inner state indirectly.

Such research implies three evolutionary patterns: (1) the first words were formed via sound symbolism of some type; (2) the transition from these to complex linguistic forms was also guided by iconicity; and (3) the latter type of iconicity is the basis of metaphor. This allows for a reframing of the metaphor hypothesis as follows: the shift from words to thoughts, from speech to language, has left its iconic traces in language, many of which are traceable to the early riddles. In this scenario, gesture fits in as, itself, an iconic mode of understanding. As David McNeill (1992, 2005) has abundantly illustrated, gesture forms and vocal forms constitute a "co-speech" system, alluding to the origins of speech as a co-occurrent gestural-vocal phenomenon. He also offers insights into how metaphor guides this system latently to this day. For example, he names some gestures as *metaphoric* gesticulants, which are iconic in abstract or conceptual ways. McNeill observed a speaker who was talking about a cartoon simultaneously raise up his hands as if he were offering a kind of object to his listener. The action represented the cartoon as if it were an object that he offered to the listener. This type of gesticulant is the counterpart of conceptual metaphors such as *presenting an idea*, *putting forth an idea*, *offering advice*, and so on, which instantiate the conceptual metaphor *ideas are conduits*, as discussed in chapter 4. This connection between gesture, speech, and metaphor, via iconicity, may well be the originating system for language.

As mentioned in chapter 1, the connection among these three modalities was discussed by the eighteenth-century philosopher Jean Jacques Rousseau (1966). In the same epoch, Vico too saw gesture as a creative force. To reiterate here how he put it, "the first language in the first mute times of the nations must have begun with signs, whether gestures or physical objects, which had natural relations to the ideas to be expressed (Bergin and Fisch 1984, 114).

The end point of the origin scenario hypothesized here is the emergence of metaphor as an ontological iconic process connecting things into complex thoughts. The root (primary) metaphors became entrenched in language via riddles and myths, which embedded the first image schemas—for instance, the action of giving things via the hands became the *conduit* image schema, the action of going somewhere to find something meaningful became the source of the *journey* image schema, and so on.

## RIDDLES AND CONSCIOUSNESS

The notion of consciousness is a slippery one, as discussed in chapter 3. A practical way to understand it is to relate it to the transition from speech to language, which must have produced an early awareness of the power of words to evoke abstract thoughts, not just name things. Following Reddy (chapter 4), language is thus a container model of consciousness itself, connected to the awareness of things contained in words and other linguistic structures—hence the importance of metaphor and riddles. When solving a riddle, we are impelled to think about the meanings of the words and the associations of sense that they entail. Consider the following well-known riddles:

> It is colored red, blue, purple, and green, as anyone can easily see, yet no one can touch it or even reach it.
> (*Answer*: a rainbow)
>
> It belongs to you, but others use it more than you do.
> (*Answer*: your name)

> What can travel around the world while staying in a corner?
> (*Answer*: a stamp)
>
> What has hands but cannot clap?
> (*Answer*: a clock)
>
> What gets wetter and wetter the more it dries?
> (*Answer*: a towel)

To arrive at the answers, the solver has to figure out how the content relates to something that appears to be impossible or unimaginable. Now, when the answer is achieved, or revealed, the reaction is what psychologists call the "aha moment," which is a rudimentary form of consciousness (Kounios and Beeman 2009). In other words, the riddles impel us to consciously reflect on (1) how the words mean what they mean, (2) how they allude to things rather than just refer to them, and (3) what aspect of a referent they bring to light that may not have been obvious. The first riddle makes an indirect comment on something that we may have not considered previously—namely that a rainbow can be seen but not touched. The one below brings out a fact about names that is true but that may also have escaped our attention. It constitutes a kind of ontological comment on the nature of names and their functions in microcosm. The remaining riddles provide perspectives on common objects that certainly would not have, under normal conditions, caught our attention. Overall, the riddles provide a mental pictography of things and concepts, providing perspectives that stimulate reflection. And this is arguably the reason why they produce the "aha" moment.

A study by Jing Luo and Kazuhisa Niki (2003) lends support to this thesis. The researchers recorded the brain activity that occurs while solving riddles using fMRIs. The participants were given a series of Japanese riddles and asked to rate their impressions on a scale based on the following prompts: (1) I understand the riddle and know the answer; (2) I understand the question, but I do not know the answer; (3) I do not understand the question and do not know the answer. This allowed the researchers to examine the brain activity of those subjects who had an "aha" moment upon viewing the answer to the riddle, versus other subjects. An example of the type of riddle used in the study is the following:

> What is it that can move heavy logs but cannot move a small nail.
> (*Answer:* a river).

Participants were given three minutes to answer this riddle, before the answer was revealed to them. The fMRI results showed that those subjects who reached the answer, showed a significant increase in activity in the right hippocampus, attributed to the formation of new associations between existing nodes. The hippocampus has been found to be involved in consciousness (Behrendt 2013; Postle 2016). It is logical to assume that the same kind of consciousness-evocation occurred when early people were presented with riddles, either to solve or to contemplate in terms of their attendant myths. This means that riddles, metaphor, and consciousness are co-occurrent. While consciousness could have emerged before riddling, it is certainly evident in it. Since a solution involves activity in the right hemisphere, there are three main conclusions that can be drawn vis-à-vis riddles: (1) they emanate in the right hemisphere, where image schemas appear to be formed; (2) the right hemisphere is thus where metaphor is programmed initially; (3) before the left hemisphere structures it linguistically, creating a bilateral system of understanding (Kacinic and Chiarello 2016).

It can thus be claimed that the early riddles and myths were themselves the means through which root metaphors were ensconced into consciousness, coming latent modes of thought as language evolved. So, for example, the Babylonian riddle of the schoolhouse as a container of knowledge and a source of intellectual vision involves several image schemas, as discussed (chapter 4), that have become first-order ones. The riddle is born of experience with schoolhouses, which constitutes an event structure. Then, through the imagination, this produces the relevant image schemas (the container, vision, the conduit, and the animal one), which become source domains that are mapped via metaphor onto the schoolhouse. This leads to an awareness (consciousness) of the importance of school, which is the riddle's solution (see Figure 5.1).

When the solution is reached, the "aha" moment itself produces a sort of "aesthetic effect" (Danesi 2002), akin to the sense of appreciation gained from artistic or musical works. This suggests that riddles stimulate various areas of the brain, not just the hemispheres but also the limbic system. The degree of aesthetic effect can be formulated in terms of a relative index—an index that varies from person to person. For example, the Riddle of the Sphinx produces a relatively high aesthetic index because the unexpected answer affects us in ways that are similar to how a beautiful melody or work

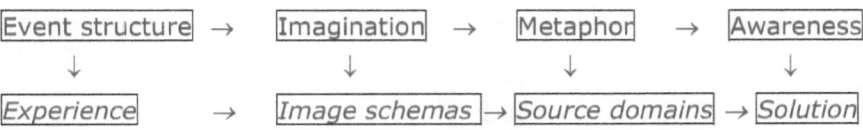

**Figure 5.1 A Model of Riddle Solving.**
*Source*: Marcel Danesi

of pictorial art do. A lower index can be seen in some pedagogical riddles that play on words in some ludic way.

The end result of the process above is awareness of something. As this becomes part of language, it generates a different state of mind called cognition by psychologists (chapter 3). The relation of consciousness to cognition was examined insightfully by philosopher Karl Popper (1976; Popper and Eccles 1977). Popper explained the emergence of consciousness in terms of three levels, which he called "Worlds." These can be adopted and adapted to provide a kind of similar modeling of a consciousness-to-cognition shift. "World 1" is the initial sense of physical objects and states controlled by neuronal synapses transmitting messages along nerve paths that cause muscles to contract or limbs to move. It involves the ability to imagine scenarios of reality as connected to each other. "World 2" is the level at which consciousness of language as a container of thoughts occurs, leading to a fairly stable cognitive state of mind. "World 3" is the level of knowledge in the objective sense, allowing the mind to understand things in abstract ways via language and to imprint it into communal memory. World 1 can be seen to correspond to the sense impressions that are encoded in speech forms via nomination—it also displays how the imagination (Vico's *fantasia*) might enter into the scene to connect the speech forms into complex thoughts. In semiotic theory, this is what Charles Peirce (1931) called *firstness*—the level at which iconic forms are forged. World 2 is anchored in a fledgling form of consciousness, where the *ingegno* enters the scene to produce root metaphors. This corresponds to Peirce's *secondness* level, which involves indexicality, the correlation of elements to each other in a specific way. World 3 coincides with the level of cognition, based on language, which allows for an encoding of thoughts into communal memory. Peirce called this *thirdness*—the level at which symbolism emerges to guide cultural systems (see Table 5.2).

Animals also have a form of consciousness, reacting purposefully to stimuli. The problem is trying to determine to what extent it intersects or coincides with human consciousness. As von Uexküll (1909) cogently argued, it is unlikely that we will ever be able to "know" how animals "know," given our different anatomical and neurological systems. Moreover, it is highly unlikely that we will ever be able to penetrate the workings of our own mind to discover how metaphors form the ontological substrate of consciousness. As argued in this book, the only way is via the "black-box" method, whereby we can infer what consciousness is by examining its products—root metaphors—which transform the world of sense into a world of meaning, by giving names to abstract experiences, via source domains, as Benjamin Lee Whorf (1941, 75) also maintained:

**Table 5.2 Parallel Views of Levels**

| Popper | Vico | Peirce |
|---|---|---|
| World 1<br>Instinctual responses evolve into raw consciousness of things | *Fantasia*<br>Ability to imagine things as transcending the instincts and as connected ontologically | Firstness<br>Ability to refer to the world via iconicity, that is, via forms that bear resemblance to their referents |
| World 2<br>Raw consciousness becomes reflection as language emerges to encode complex thoughts. | *Ingegno*<br>The products of the imagination are converted into metaphors, establishing ontological connections among referents. | Secondness<br>This is the level at which indexicality emerges as a relational form of reference and understanding. |
| World 3<br>Consciousness becomes embedded habitually into everyday communal sense-making via symbolic systems, including language. | *Memoria*<br>Consciousness becomes habitualized as the sense of history shifts from mythic and legendary to prosaic. | Thirdness<br>This is the level at which symbolism dominates habitual forms of thought. |

Our metaphorical system, by naming nonspatial experiences after spatial ones, imputes to sounds, smells, tastes, emotions, and thoughts qualities like the colors, luminosities, shapes, angles, textures, and motions of spatial experience. And to some extent the reverse transference occurs; for, after much talking about tones as high, low, sharp, dull, heavy, brilliant, slow, the talker finds it easy to think of some factors in spatial experience as like factors of tone. Thus we speak of "tones" of color, a gray "monotone," a "loud" necktie, a "taste" in dress: all spatial metaphor in reverse.

## BICAMERAL MIND THEORY

The foregoing discussion leads to a consideration of bicameral mind theory, as proposed by Julian Jaynes (1976), which, although it has evoked various critical responses, is nonetheless a relevant one for the present purposes, since it explicitly relates the origin of language to metaphor, consciousness, and cognition. Jaynes's key notion is that the two chambers of the hominid brain became interconnected at some evolutionary point to produce conceptual language, whereby the brain became bilateral with separated hemispheres. As neuroscientific research on the hemispheres has established, the right one is involved initially in the processing of image schemas and metaphors, while the left one is involved in other language functions, including the stabilization of conceptual metaphors into semantic categories (Schmidt and Seger 2009;

Diaz, Barrett, and Hogstrom 2011; Lai, van Dam, Conant, Binder, and Rutvik 2015). This conceptual flow from right to left matches the evolutionary flow of consciousness to cognition discussed above, with riddles and myths being among the first documentations of how this flow became imprinted in early language forms.

As Jaynes (1976, 38) put it, "if consciousness is based on language, then it follows that only humans are conscious, and that we became so at some historical epoch after language was evolved." Like the philological method used in this book, Jaynes searched ancient texts for early evidence of the language-consciousness nexus, even tracing Greek words for mind back to their metaphorical origins. Riddles were not in Jaynes's etymological database, but these can only further support and strengthen his theory. As language subserved early ontological functions, it gradually evolved into cognitive states, as distinct from, but phylogenetically related to, metaphorical consciousness. As Jaynes (1976, 45) succinctly put it, consciousness arises "from language, and specifically from metaphor." Cognition is the system of thoughts encoded by language; consciousness is the imaginative state of mind that leads to language but can precede or transcend it. The difference between the two states is a blurry one, since there is much overlap between them (Gulick 2012; Brown 2014). For the present purposes, consciousness can be constrained to mean awareness of something in the world or in the mind—as for example the notion of destiny—and cognition can be constrained to mean the ways in which metaphor circumscribes the awareness in specific terms—such as *journeys*, *paths*, and so forth. In other words, it gives consciousness a specific shape.

Bicameral mentality is nonconscious, or more accurately preconscious. The breakdown of bicamerality into bilateral hemisphericity, Jaynes argued, occurred when metaphor and its narrative products appeared on the human evolutionary timetable. If Jaynes is right, and the evidence he puts forth in support of his theory is substantial, then it supports the metaphor hypothesis, and vice versa, the metaphor hypothesis supports Jaynes's overall perspective. Jaynes built his case that human brains existed in a bicameral state until as recently as 3,000 years ago by citing philological evidence, as mentioned. Until Homer's *Iliad*, he suggested, humans did not possess self-awareness. Rather, the bicameral mind was guided by inner images of "gods" commanding them to act in specific ways, paralleling Vico's age of the gods (chapter 3). Jaynes speculates that bicameral mentality began "breaking down" during the second millennium BCE, when metaphorical language emerged as a system of cognition.

The parallels with Vico are striking. What is missing from Jaynes's approach is any discussion of the mechanism that emerged to facilitate the transition from bicameral speech to bilateral language—namely, poetic logic:

The authors of this poetry were the first peoples, whom we find to have been all theological poets, who without doubt, as we are told, founded the gentile nations with fables of the gods. And here, by the principles of this new critical art ... the first men ... imagined first such and such gods and then such and such others. The natural theogony or generation of the gods, formed naturally in the minds of these first men, may give us a rational chronology of the poetic history of the gods. (Bergin and Fisch 1984, 6)

In the citation, *authors* refers to the first speakers, and *poetry* to metaphorical language. The *fables of the gods* were the founding mythic narratives. The images of gods as human figures likely came about, as Jaynes explains, because one chamber of the mind was "speaking" to the other chamber, which listened and obeyed. The inner "speaking" likely produced hallucinations, which became the basis for early images of the gods. It was metaphor that integrated the two chambers into interacting hemispheres. At that point, language emerged as a bilateral, rather than bicameral, faculty of the whole integrated brain.

Mark Johnson (1987) has provided an insightful description of how image schemas provide evidence of the transition from consciousness, based on experience, to cognition via metaphorical mapping. For instance, the container schema, as a spatially bounded landmark, is at the source of the various meanings of the word *out*:

> She went *out* of the room.
> He got *out* of the car.
> Out dog jumped *out* of the pen.

The same word might indicate a mass that spreads externally from the containing landmark:

> Your friend poured *out* the beans.
> Roll *out* the carpet.
> Send *out* the troops.

There are other uses, of course, including connotative extensions, but the container image schema unites them all conceptually. Expressions such as *think up*, *think over*, and *think through*, discussed previously (chapter 4), support this model of image schematic conceptualization, since these are based on image schemas that connect ideas to objects and their movement through bounded spaces, via layering processes (as discussed). It is clear that cognition cannot be separated from image-schematic structure.

## SUMMARIZING THE METAPHOR HYPOTHESIS

The metaphor hypothesis—the claim that metaphor is the core of language and that it appears in the early riddles and myths—can be summarized schematically as follows. Bicameral mind theory, together with the flow model put forth in this chapter, suggests that poetic logic was the mechanism that led to full-blown language and that its most "luminous product," as Vico called it, is metaphor. Poetic logic is part of human ingenuity, while poetic wisdom is embedded in the imagination. In the *New Science*, Vico suggested that these innate faculties of the brain helped conscious humans cope with the first stages of social life, leading to the emergence of language. As he understood, metaphors, by definition, are not literally true. They are fictions, or fables to use both Vico's and Vygotsky's (1962) term. But it is through these fictions that we grasp reality on our own terms. The Riddle of the Sphinx is a fiction—days and life phases are really not the same. It has been constructed in such a way as to represent a sequence of events that are felt to be logically connected to each other or causally intertwined in some way.

The narrative structure of riddles and myths is felt, to this day, to reflect the structure of real-life events, establishing a point of view for making judgments about moral, philosophical, or social problems. Myths are also the source of early (founding) symbols. The Greeks symbolized the sun as the god Helios driving a flaming chariot across the sky. The Egyptians represented the sun as a boat. Animals, human beings, and plants have all stood as symbols for ideas and events in myths of all kinds, imprinted in specific source domains. In Babylonian mythology, the *journey* metaphor is prominent, alongside the image schema of magical plants, whereby the hero Gilgamesh searched for a special herb that made anyone who ate it immortal.

Needless to say, such arguments do not empirically establish metaphor, riddles, and myths as evidence of language origins. But they are highly plausible as part of an origins scenario, as discussed throughout this book. The metaphor hypothesis, when considered from an overall perspective suggests that speech and language are connected via iconicity at various levels, from the phonic to the ontological. The metaphor hypothesis suggests that consciousness emerged in the context of the early riddles and myths, which introduced root metaphors and their corresponding source domains into language—as the philological evidence strongly suggests. After this occurred, language introduced cognitive units of understanding, which became embedded in grammar and semantics, forging communal memory (see Figure 5.2).

Roman Jakobson adopted two tropes as fundamental in the production of conceptual language—metaphor and metonymy—corresponding to iconic and indexical language. As Hayden White (1973) suggests, this is in line

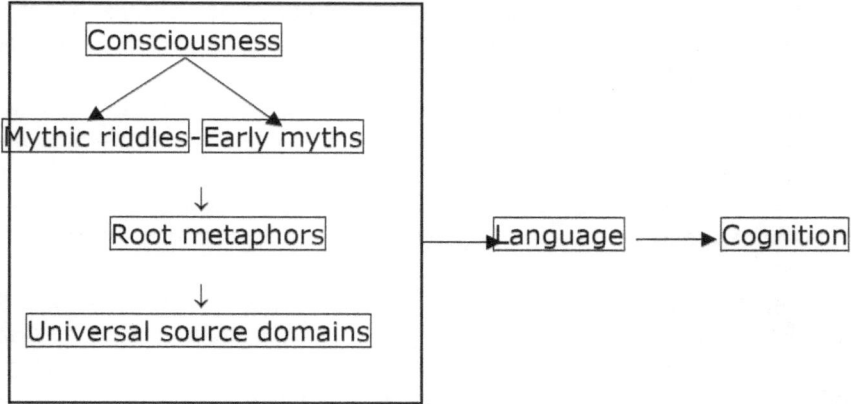

**Figure 5.2 The Metaphor Hypothesis.**
*Source:* Marcel Danesi

with Vichian theory, even though it lacks the final phase in the language scenario, consisting of prose and irony. Jakobson actually found evidence for this flow in the pathology of speech, whereby the available data in his era pointed to two types of aphasia, based on what he called "similarity disorder" (metaphor) and "contiguity disorder" (metonymy; Jakobson and Halle 1956, 67–96). Aphasics with the former disorder had difficulty selecting the word they wanted, such as saying *pencil sharpener* when they meant *knife*, or *knife* when they meant *fork* (Jakobson and Halle 1956, 79, 83). Aphasics with contiguity disorder had difficulty combining words correctly and used quasi-metaphorical expressions, such as calling a *microscope* a *spyglass* (Jakobson and Halle 1956, 86).

The metaphor hypothesis has been based on philological riddle data, which overall supports the various aspects of conceptual metaphor theory, as discussed throughout this book, validating Lakoff's (1979) overall view of metaphor as a faculty of mind, not just of language:

> The general theory of metaphor is given by characterizing such cross-domain mappings. And in the process, everyday abstract concepts like time, states, change, causation, and purpose also turn out to be metaphorical. The result is that metaphor (that is, cross-domain mapping) is absolutely central to ordinary natural language semantics.

The semantic-conceptual system of a language contains thousands of conceptual metaphors—mappings from one domain to another. How these originated and why has been the theme of this book. The evidence for the emergence of the primary (root) source domains mapped onto language comes from riddles and myths, mainly because these are documented archeologically and can thus be accessed and analyzed accordingly. The riddle evidence also indicates that, as they gained different social functions, riddling adopted new types of mappings, including metonymic and ironic ones (chapter 4).

Perhaps one of the most significant findings emerging from the examination of early riddles is the omnipresence of specific image schemas—the *container*, the *conduit*, *phases*, *journeys*, and so on. The corollary to the metaphor hypothesis is that language is not a direct biological endowment—speech is. It is a human construction based on poetic logic and its ingenuity (literally). It also entails that increasingly complex cognition is the result of the higher-order layering of source domains. Layering may also be the source of grammar and complex semantics, as discussed in chapter 3. Riddles and myths are the first testaments of the use of syntax to coordinate thoughts in a conscious way. Indeed, one cannot solve riddles without employing a conscious mode of understanding the words and their organization. Immanuel Kant (1790, 278) saw language as connected to the brain's ability to synthesize scattered bits of information into holistic entities that can then be analyzed reflectively. Kant's ideas found their implicit elaboration and amplification in Charles Peirce's *Existential Graph Theory* (Peirce 1931–1956, volume 2, 398–433; volume 4, 347–584), which showed how grammar involves relations that can be graphed iconically. Therefore, a sentence is a sort of mapping of one group of relations onto another, displaying the essential nature of something in a holistic visual way. Peirce called his graphs "moving pictures of thought" (Peirce, volume 4, 8–11) because in their structure we can literally "see" how a given idea is organized.

## EPILOGUE

The Riddle of the Sphinx was the starting point for examining the metaphor hypothesis; it is also an end point. Its conceptual metaphorical structure is connected ontologically to the Oedipus myth as follows:

- Oedipus pursues a goal—to find out who he is—by undertaking a journey (to Thebes). The image schema of a journey as the way to self-discovery has since permeated the traditions and literatures of the world—from the journey of Odysseus in Homer's *Odyssey* and Dante's journey into the *inferno* in his *Divina commedia*, to Jack Kerouac's *On the Road*, among myriad others.
- Metaphorical journeys always present obstacles or impediments to be overcome—Oedipus runs unwittingly into his father along the way, who blocks his way to Thebes, having to kill him in order to continue.

- The end of the journey leads to the desired goal—self-discovery, which in the case of Oedipus is actually a disaster.

Metaphors cross conceptual boundaries, creating layers of mappings that accrue over time to form the basis of knowledge and understanding. As Lakoff (1979) has put it, "Each mapping is a fixed pattern of conceptual correspondences across conceptual domains . . . [and] defines an open-ended class of potential correspondences across inference patterns." In effect, the image schemas in the Sphinx's Riddle and the Oedipus myth are mapped onto several layers of conceptualization, criss-crossing ontologically, showing how abstract thinking likely emerged on the basis of the super positioning of image schemas, which congeal into thought modes. Lakoff (1979) has termed this the invariance principle (as discussed):

> The Invariance Principle claims that what we had called propositional structure is really image-schematic structure. In other words: So-called propositional inferences arise from the inherent topological structure of the image-schemas mapped by metaphor onto concepts like time, states, changes, actions, causes, purposes, means, quantity, and categories. . . . If the Invariance Principle is correct, it has a remarkable consequence, namely that: Abstract reasoning is a special case of imaged-based reasoning. Image-based reasoning is fundamental and abstract reasoning is image-based reasoning under metaphorical projections to abstract domains.

The key part in Sophocles's *Oedipus Rex* is the Sphinx's Riddle, even though the actual riddle is never articulated in the play, just mentioned by allusion. This reveals that the audiences already knew the riddle quite well. Quite a few versions of the riddle preceded the play, from both oral traditions and the theater, such as in plays by Apollodorus and Athenaeus, which were widely known society-wide (Frazer 1921; Braund and Wilkins 2000):

> *Apollodorus's Version*:
> What is that which has one voice and yet becomes four-footed and two-footed and three-footed?
>
> *Athenaeus's Version:*
> A thing there is whose voice is one;
> Whose feet are four and two and three.

The latter may be the oldest written version of the riddle, since it is in dactylic hexameter, one of the earliest poetic structures of ancient Greece. Mentions of the riddle also appeared in a lost play by Aeschylus, and in Euripides's play *Oedipus*. The use of *voice* in the two versions above is rather significant—it is itself a metaphor for language. Also, changes in the physical voice match the three ages of life—infants have a high tone, adults a deeper tone, and older persons have a more brittle voice.

The choice of a sphinx to present the riddle to humans is also a metaphorical strategy. The source domain in this case is the Egyptian *shesepankh*, which means "divine or living image" (Bauer 2007, 110–112), initially referring to the statue of the creature with the head of a human and the body of a lion that was carved out of "living rock," rather than to the beast itself. Sphinxes appear near the tombs of pharaohs, perhaps to indicate their close relationship with the deity, Sekhmet, who was a lioness.

The story of Oedipus has inspired an infinitude of writers, philosophers, artists, and scholars. In Jean Cocteau's *The Infernal Machine* (1932), the Sphinx actually gives the answer of her riddle to Oedipus so that she can be freed from killing others and killing herself, eventually returning to the heavens from whence she came. But in all versions, there is an underlying ontological concept—the human condition is what it is, to use a Buddhist principle. All we can do is describe it via metaphor so that we can better grasp it on our own terms. As Vico constantly emphasized, metaphor is our best clue for understanding the origin of human thought, language, and culture. And that clue can be found hidden in the early riddles and myths.

# References

Aarne, Antii. 1918. *Vergleichende Rätselforschungen*, 3 vols. Helsinki: Suomalainen Tiedeakatemia.

Abrahams, Roger D. 1972. "The Literary Study of the Riddle." *Texas Studies in Literature and Language* 14: 177–197.

Akínyẹmí, Akíntúndé. 2015. *Orature and Yorùbá Riddles*. New York: Palgrave Macmillan.

Alcuin. *Lectures Delivered in the Cathedral Church of Bristol*. Internet Archive, https://archive.org/stream/alcuinofyorklect00brow/alcuinofyorklect00brow_djvu.txt.

Aldhelm. *The Riddles of Aldhelm*. https://archive.org/details/riddlesofaldhelm0000aldh.

Alster, B. 1976. "A Sumerian Riddle Collection." *Journal of Near Eastern Studies* 35: 263–267.

Aristotle. 1952a. *Rhetoric*. W. D. Ross, ed. *The Works of Aristotle*, Vol. 11. Oxford: Clarendon Press.

Aristotle. 1952b. *Poetics*. W. D. Ross ed. *The Works of Aristotle*, Vol. 11. Oxford: Clarendon Press.

Arnheim, Rudolf. 1969. *Visual Thinking*. Berkeley: University of California Press.

Asch, Solomon. 1950. "On the Use of Metaphor in the Description of Persons." In H. Werner ed., *On Expressive Language*, pp. 86–94. Worcester: Clark University Press.

Bar-Hillel, Maya, Noah, Tom, and Frederick, Shane. 2018. "Learning Psychology from Riddles: The Case of Stumpers." *Judgment and Decision Making* 13: 112–122.

Barrick, Mac E. 1974. The Newspaper Riddle Joke. *The Journal of American Folklore* 87: 253–257.

Baudrillard, Jean. 1987. *The Ecstasy of Communication*. St. Louis: Telos Press.

Beckby, Hermann. 1968. *Anthologia Graeca*. Munich: Heimeran.

Becker, Alton L. 2000 *Beyond Translation: Essays toward a Modern Philology*. Ann Arbor: University of Michigan Press.

Behrendt, Ralf-Peter. 2013. "Hippocampus and Consciousness." *Review of Neuroscience* 24: 239–266.

Bergin, Thomas G., and Fisch, Max. 1984. *The New Science of Giambattista Vico*. Ithaca: Cornell University Press.

Berrington, Benj. S., and Berrington, John S. 1905. *English Riddles: With Explanations and Notes in Dutch*. Purmerendm: J. Muusses.
Bickerton, Derek. 2014. *More Than Nature Needs: Language, Mind, and Evolution*. Cambridge: Harvard University Press.
Black, Max. 1962. *Models and Metaphors*. Ithaca: Cornell University Press.
Bauer, S. Wise. 2007. *The History of the Ancient World*. New York: W. W. Norton.
Bomhard, Allan R. 1992. "The Nostratic Macrofamily." *Word* 43: 61–84.
Braund, David, and Wilkins, John. 2000. *Athenaeus and His World: Reading Greek Culture in the Roman Empire*. Exeter: University of Exeter Press.
British Word Puzzles. Digital Commons, https://digitalcommons.butler.edu/cgi/viewcontent.cgi?article=1737&context=wordways.
Brown, Richard. 2014. "Consciousness Doesn't Overflow Cognition." *Frontiers in Psychology* 4: https://doi.org/10.3389/fpsyg.2014.01399.
Brown, Roger W. 1958. *Words and Things*. New York: The Free Press.
Brown, Roger, Black, Abraham, and Horowitz, Arnold. 1955. "Phonetic Symbolism in Natural Languages." *Journal of Abnormal and Social Psychology* 50: 388–393.
Bühler, Karl. 1908 [1951]. "On Thought Connection." In D. Rapaport, ed., *Organization and Pathology of Thought*, pp. 81–92. New York: Columbia University Press.
Burrows, Hannah. 2014. "Wit and Wisdom: The Worldview of the Old Norse-Icelandic Riddles and their Relationship to Eddic Poetry." In: Martin Chase, ed., *Eddic, Skaldic, and Beyond: Poetic Variety in Medieval Iceland and Nor*way, pp. 114–135. New York: Fordham University Press.
Campbell, Joseph. 1972. *Myths to Live By*. Harmondsworth: Penguin.
Carroll, Lewis. *The Complete Works of Lewis Carroll*, Internet Archive: https://archive.org/details/completeworksofl1920carr.
Carroll, Lewis. 1865. *Alice's Adventures in Wonderland*. London: Macmillan.
Carroll, Lewis. 1869. *Phantasmagoria, and Other Poems*. London: Macmillan.
Carroll, Lewis. 1871. *Through the Looking-Glass, and What Alice Found There*. London: Macmillan.
Carroll, Lewis. 1883. *Rhyme? and Reason?* London: Macmillan.
Cassirer, Ernst. 1953. *Language and Myth*. New York: Dover.
Castel, Bertrand du. 2015. "Pattern Activation/Recognition Theory of Mind." *Frontiers in Computational Neuroscience* 9: doi:10.3389/fncom.2015.00090.
Castiglione, Baldassare. 1528. *Il libro del cortegiano*. Venice: d'Aldo Romano.
Chambers, R. W., Förster, Max, and Flower, Robin. 1933. *The Exeter Book of Old English Poetry*. London: P. Lund.
Chiaro, Delia. 1992. *The Language of Jokes: Analysing Verbal Play*. London: Routledge.
Chomsky, Noam. 1957. *Syntactic Structures*. The Hague: Mouton.
Chomsky, Noam. 1965. *Aspects of the Theory of Syntax*. Cambridge: MIT Press.
Cicero 1942. *De Oratore*, trans. by E. W. Sutton and H. Rackham. Cambridge: Harvard University Press.
Clay, Jenny Strauss. 2003. *Hesiod's Cosmos*. Cambridge: Cambridge University Press.

Cole, K. C. 1985. *Sympathetic Vibrations*. New York: Bantam.
Connor, Kathleen and Kogan, Nathan. 1980. "Topic-Vehicle Relations in Metaphor: The Issue of a Symmetry." In Richard P. Honeck and Robert R. Hoffman, eds., *Cognition and Figurative Language*, pp. 238–308. Hillsdale, NJ: Lawrence Erlbaum Associates.
Cook, Eleanor. 2009. *Enigmas and Riddles in Literature*. Cambridge: Cambridge University Press.
Currie, Thomas E., Meade, Andrew, Guillon, Myrtille, and Mace, Ruth. 2013. "Cultural Phylogeography of the Bantu Languages of Sub–Saharan Africa." *Royal Society Publishing*. https://doi.org/10.1098/rspb.2013.0695.
Dahl, Christoph D., and Adachi, Ikuma. 2013. "Conceptual Metaphorical Mapping in Chimpanzees." *Pan troglodytes. eLife* 2: doi:10.7554/eLife.00932.
Damasio, Antonio R. 1994. *Descartes' Error: Emotion, Reason, and the Human Brain*. New York: G. P. Putnam's.
Danesi, Marcel. 1993. *Vico, Metaphor, and the Origin of Language*. Bloomington: Indiana University Press.
Danesi, Marcel. 2001. "Layering Processes in Metaphorization." *International Journal of Computing Anticipatory Systems* 8, 2001: 157–173.
Danesi, Marcel. 2002. *The Puzzle Instinct: The Meaning of Puzzles in Human Life*. Bloomington: Indiana University Press.
Danesi, Marcel. 2003. *Second Language Teaching: A View from the Right Side of the Brain*. Dordrecht: Kluwer.
Danesi, Marcel. 2004. *Poetic Logic: The Role of Metaphor in Thought, Language, and Culture*. Madison: Atwood Press.
Danesi, Marcel. 2007. *The Quest for Meaning: A Guide to Semiotic Theory and Practice*. Toronto: University of Toronto Press.
Danesi, Marcel. 2013. *Discovery in Mathematics*. Munich: Lincom Europa.
Danesi, Marcel. 2017. "The Bidirectionality of Metaphor." *Poetics Today* 38: 15–33.
Danesi, Marcel. 2018. *Ahmes' Legacy: Puzzles and the Mathematical Mind*. New York: Springer.
Danesi, Marcel. 2019. "Una nota sull'uso didattico dell'indovinello linguistico." *Italica* 96: 331–342.
Danesi, Marcel. 2020. *Curious History of the Riddle*. New York: Quarto Press.
Davis, Paul J., and Hersh, Reuben. 1986. *Descartes' Dream: The World According to Mathematics*. Boston: Houghton Mifflin.
De Bono, Edward. 1970. *Lateral Thinking: Creativity Step-by-Step*. New York: Harper & Row.
Deekshitar, Raja. 2004. "Discovering the Anthropomorphic Lion in Indian Art." *Marg, A Magazine of the Arts* 55: 34–41.
Demisch, Heinz. 1977. *Die Sphinx. Geschichte ihrer Darstellung von den Anfangen bis zur Gegenwart*. Stuttgart: Urachhaus Verlag.
Descartes, René. 1637. *Essaies philosophiques*. Leyden: L'imprimerie de Ian Maire.
Diamond, Arthur A. 1959. *The History and Origin of Language*. New York: Philosophical Library.

Diaz, Michele T., Barrett, Kyle M., and Hogstrom, Larson J. 2011. "The Influence of Sentence Novelty and Figurativeness on Brain Activity." *Neuropsychologia* 49: 320–330.

Doumas, Leonidas, Hummel, John, and Sandhofer, Catherine. 2008. "A Theory of the Discovery and Predication of Relational Concepts." *Psychological Review* 115: 1–43.

Dundes, Alan. 1963. "Towards a Structural Definition of the Riddle." *Journal of American Folklore* 76: 111–118.

Durkheim, Émile. 1912. *The Elementary Forms of Religious Life*. New York: Collier.

Eco, Umberto. 1984. *Semiotics and the Philosophy of Language*. Bloomington: Indiana University Press.

Eco, Umberto. 1989. *The Open Work*. Cambridge: Harvard University Press.

Eco, Umberto. 1990. *The Limits of Interpretation*. Bloomington: Indiana University Press.

Edie, James M. 1976. *Speaking and Meaning: The Phenomenology of Language*. Bloomington: Indiana University Press.

Edmunds, Lowell. 1981. *The Sphinx in the Oedipus Legend*. Hain: Königstein im Taunus.

Eliade, Mircea. 1961. *The Sacred and the Profane: The Nature of Religion*. New York: Harper Torchbooks.

Emantian, Michele. 1995. "Metaphor and the Expression of Emotion: The Value of Cross-Cultural Perspectives." *Metaphor and Symbolic Activity* 10: 163–182.

Epley, Nicholas, Waytz, Adam, and Cacioppo, John T. 2007. "On Seeing Human: A Three-Factor Theory of Anthropomorphism." *Psychological Review*: 864–886.

Ervas, Francesca, Rossi, Maria Grazia, Ojha, Amitash, and Indurkhya, Bipin. 2021. "The Double Framing Effect of Emotive Metaphors in Argumentation." *Frontiers in Psychology*: doi:10.3389/fpsyg.2021.628460.

Everett, Daniel L. 2019. *How Language Began*. New York: Liveright.

*Exeter Book*. Internet Archive, https://archive.org/details/exeterbook0000unse.

Fairon, Pat. 1992. *Irish Riddles*. San Francisco: Chronicle Books.

Faizullina, Nailya Ivanovna, Zamaletdinov, Radif Rifkatovich, and Fattakhova, Nailya Nuryjhanovna. 2020. "Metaphor Analysis in The Russian Riddle as a Secondary Nomination Source." *Journal of Research in Applied Linguistics* 11: https://rals.scu.ac.ir/article_16288_33e6bbaf0303c726411c116aca281c2e.pdf.

Fauconnier, Gilles, and Turner, Mark. 2002. *The Way We Think: Conceptual Blending and the Mind's Hidden Complexities*. New York: Basic.

Feldman, Jerome, and Narayanan, Srinivas. 2004. "Embodied Meaning in a Neural Theory of Language." *Brain and Language* 89: 385–392.

Ferrari, Gloria. 1997. "Figures in the Text: Metaphors and Riddles in the *Agamemnon*." *Classical Philology* 92: 1–45.

Fitch, W. Tecumseh. 2012. *Evolution of Language*. Cambridge: Cambridge University Press.

Fletcher, Angus. 1991. *Colors of the Mind: Connections on Thinking in Literature*. Cambridge, MA: Harvard University Press.

Frazer, Sir James George. 1921. *Apollodorus: The Library*. London: William Heinemann.
Frye, Northrop. 1981. *The Great Code: The Bible and Literature*. Toronto: Academic Press.
Frye, Northrop. 1990. *Words with Power*. Harmondsworth: Penguin.
Gameson, Richard. 1996. *The Origin of the Exeter Book of Old English Poetry*. Cambridge: Cambridge University Press.
Gamkrelidze, Thomas V., and Ivanov, Vjaceslav V. 1984. *Indo-European and the Indo-Europeans: A Reconstruction and Historical Typological Analysis of a Protolanguage and Proto-Culture*. Moscow: Tblisi State University.
Gamkrelidze, Thomas V., and Ivanov, Vjaceslav V. 1990. "The Early History of Indo-European Languages." *Scientific American* 262: 110–116.
Gardner, Howard. 1982. *Art, Mind, and Brain: A Cognitive Approach to Creativity*. New York: Basic.
Gardner, Martin. 1996. *The Universe in a Handkerchief: Lewis Carroll's Mathematical Recreations, Games, Puzzles, and Word Plays*. London: Copernicus.
Geary, James. 2011. "Metaphors in Mind." *The Macmillan Dictionary Blog*. https://www.macmillandictionaryblog.com/metaphors-in-mind.
Gentner, Dedre. 1983. "Structure Mapping: A Theoretical Framework for Analogy." *Cognitive Science* 7: 155–170.
Georges, Robert A., and Dundes, Alan. 1963. "Toward a Structural Definition of the Riddle." *The Journal of American Folklore* 76: 111–118.
Gibbs, Raymond. 2000. "Making Good Psychology Out of Blending Theory." *Cognitive Linguistics* 11: 347–358.
Gibbs, Raymond. 2017. *Metaphor Wars: Conceptual Metaphors in Human Life*. Cambridge: Cambridge University Press.
Glicksohn, Joseph. 2001. "Metaphor and Consciousness: The Path Less Taken." *The Journal of Mind and Behavior* 22: 343–363.
Gordon, Edmund I. 1960. "A New Look at the Wisdom of Sumer and Akkad." *Bibliotheca Orientalis* 17: 122–152.
Gould, Stephen J. 1977. *Ontogeny and Phylogeny*. Cambridge: Harvard University Press.
Glucksberg, Sam, and Danks, Joseph H. 1975. *Experimental Psycholinguistics*. New York: John Wiley and Sons.
Grady, Joseph. 1997. *Foundations of Meaning: Primary Metaphors and Primary Scenes*. Berkeley: University of California at Berkeley.
Gray, Russell D., and Atkinson, Quentin D. 2003. "Language–Tree Divergence Times Support the Anatolian Theory of Indo-European Origin." *Nature* 425: 435–439.
Green, Thomas A., and Pepicello, William J. 1984. "The Riddle Process." *The Journal of American Folklore* 97: 189–203.
Gulere, Cornelius. 2012. *Riddle Events, Contexts and Audiences: Aesthetic Performance Record of Nsinze Seed School Riddling and Analysis of Structure of the Riddle Acts*. Riga: Lambert Academic Publishing.

Gulick, Robert van. 2012. "Consciousness and Cognition. In E. Margolis, R. Samuels, and S. P. Stich, eds., *The Oxford Handbook of Philosophy of Cognitive Science*. Oxford Handbooks Online.

Hallyn, Ferdinand. 1990. *The Poetic Structure of the World: Copernicus and Kepler*. New York: Zone Books.

Harries, Lyndon. 1971. "The Riddle in Africa." *The Journal of American Folklore* 84: 377–393.

Hart, Donn V. 1964. *Riddles in Philippine Folklore: An Anthropological Analysis*. Syracuse: Syracuse University Press.

Heesterman, J. C. 1997. "On Riddles." In P. Bhatt, ed., *Significations: Essays in Honour of Henry Schogt*, pp. 65–69. Toronto: Canadian Scholars' Press.

Heidegger, Martin. 1970. *Phaenomenologie und Theologie*. Frankfurt: Klostermann.

Henrikson, Alf. 1998. *Stora mytologiska uppslagsboken*. Bokförlaget Forum.

Hesse, Hermann. 1943. *Das Glasperlenspiel*. Frankfurt: Suhrkamp.

Hewes, Gordon W. 1973. "Primate Communication and the Gestural Origin of Language." *Current Anthropology* 14: 5–24.

Hewes, Gordon W. 1976. "The Current Status of the Gestural Theory of Language Origin." In S. R. Harnad, H. D. Steklis, and J. Lancaster, eds., *Origins and Evolution of Language and Speech*, pp. 482–504. New York: New York Academy of Sciences.

Hickman du Bois, Elizabeth. 1912. *The Hundred Riddles of Symphosius*. Woodstock: The Elm Tree Press.

Hinton, Leanne, Nichols, Johanna, and Ohala, John, eds. 1994. *Sound Symbolism*. Cambridge: Cambridge University Press.

Hobbes, Thomas. (1656) 1992. *Elements of Philosophy*. London: Molesworth.

Holyoak, Keith, and Thagard, Paul. 1995. *Mental Leaps: Analogy in Creative Thought*. Cambridge: MIT Press.

Honeck, Richard P., and Hoffman, Robert R., eds. 1980. *Cognition and Figurative Language*. Hillsdale, NJ: Lawrence Erlbaum Associates.

Hovanec, Helene. 1978. *The Puzzlers' Paradise: From the Garden of Eden to the Computer Age*. New York: Paddington Press.

Huizinga, Johan. 1938. *Homo Ludens: A Study of the Play-Element in Human Culture*. New York: Beacon Press.

Hull, Vernam, and Taylor, Archer. 1942. *A Collection of Welsh Riddles*. Berkeley: University of California Press.

Hummel, John, and Holyoak, Keith. 2005. "Relational Reasoning in a Neurally Plausible Cognitive Architecture." *Current Directions in Psychological Science* 14: 153–157.

Humour, Wit, & Satire. Internet Archive, https://archive.org/stream/gri_33125015242841/gri_33125015242841_djvu.txt.

Hurford, James R. 2014. *The Origins of Language*. Oxford: Oxford University Press.

Husserl, Edmund .1890. *Philosophie der Arithmetik*. The Hague: Nijhoff.

Hussey, Edward. 1982. "Epistemology and Meaning in Heraclitus." In M. Schofield and M. C. Nussbaum, eds., *Language and Logos*, pp. 33–59. Cambridge: Cambridge University Press.

Huxley, Francis. 1976. *The Raven and the Writing Desk.* New York: Harper and Row.
Isbell, Billie Jean, and Roncalla Fernandez, Fredy Amilcar. 1977. "The Ontogenesis of Metaphor: Riddle Games among Quechua Speakers Seen as Cognitive Discovery Procedures." *Journal of Latin American Lore* 3: 19–49.
Jakobson, Roman. 1960: "Linguistics and Poetics." In T. A. Sebeok, ed., *Style in Language*, pp. 350–377. Cambridge: MIT Press
Jakobson, Roman, and Halle, Morris. 1956: *Fundamentals of Language.* The Hague: Mouton.
Jamison, S. W., and Brereton, J. P. 2014. *The Rigveda: The Earliest Religious Poetry of India.* New York: Oxford University Press.
Jay, Peter. 1973. *The Greek Anthology and Other Ancient Greek Epigrams.* London: Allen Lane.
Jaynes, Julian. 1976. *The Origin of Consciousness in the Breakdown of the Bicameral Mind.* Boston: Houghton Mifflin.
Jespersen, Otto. 1922. *Language: Its Nature, Development and Origin.* New York: Henry Holt.
Johansson, Patrick. 2004. *Zazanilli: La palabra-enigma: Acertijos y adivinanzas de los antiguos nahuas.* Mexico: McGraw-Hill Interamericana.
Johnson, Mark. 1987. *The Body in the Mind: The Bodily Basis of Meaning, Imagination, and Reason.* Chicago: University of Chicago Press.
Jung, Carl. 1959. *The Archetypes and the Collective Unconscious.* Princeton: Princeton University Press.
Juster, A. M. 2015. *Saint Aldhelm's Riddles.* Toronto: University of Toronto Press.
Kacinic, Natalie E., and Chiarello, Christine. 2016. "Understanding Metaphors: Is the Right Hemisphere Uniquely Involved?" *Brain and Language* 100: 188–207.
Kaivola-Bregenhøj, Annikki. 2016. "Riddles: Perspectives on the Use, Function and Change in a Folklore Genre." *Studia Fennica Folkloristica*, 10. Helsinki: Finnish Literature Society, 2016.
Kaivola-Bregenhøj, Annikki. 2017. "Riddles and Humour." DOI:10.7592/FEJF2017.69.kaivola_bregenhoj.
Kang, Xiaofei. 2006. *The Cult of the Fox: Power, Gender, and Popular Religion in Late Imperial and Modern China.* New York: Columbia University Press.
Kant, Immanuel. 1790. *Critique of Pure Reason.* New York: St. Martin's.
Kaplan, Kalman. 2020. *Living a Purposeful Life.* Eugene: Wipf & Stock.
Katz, Albert N. 2008. "The Journeys of Life: Examining a Conceptual Metaphor with Semantic and Episodic Memory Recall." *Metaphor and Symbol* 23: 148–173.
Kennedy, Victoria. 2019. "Riddles and Rhymes: The Logic of Nonsense in Alice's Adventures in Wonderland." *Whitmore Rare Books.* http://whitmorerarebooks.com/pages/digest/4/riddles-and-rhymes-the-logic-of-nonsense-in.
Keyne, Peter, and Amsel, Rudolph. 2014. *The Great Book of Riddles.* Seattle: Elsinore Books.
Köngas-Maranda, Elli. 1976. "Riddles and Riddling: An Introduction." *The Journal of American Folklore* 89: 127–137.

Kounios, John, and Beeman, Mark. 2009. "The *Aha* Moment: The Cognitive Neuroscience of Insight." *Current Directions in Psychological Science*: https://journals.sagepub.com/doi/full/10.1111/j.1467-8721.2009.01638.x.

Kövecses, Zoltán. 2002. *Metaphor: A Practical Introduction.* Oxford: Oxford University Press.

Kövecses, Zoltán. 2020. *Extended Conceptual Metaphor Theory.* Cambridge: Cambridge University Press.

Korzybski, Alfred. 1921. *Manhood of Humanity: The Science and Art of Human Engineering.* New York: Dutton.

Krantz, Grover S. 1988. "Laryngeal Descent in 40,000 Year Old Fossils." In M. E. Landsberg, ed., *The Genesis of Language*, pp. 173–180. Berlin: Mouton de Gruyter.

Lacan, Jacques. 1977. *Écrits.* London: Routledge.

Lai, Vicky T., van Dam, Wessel, Conant, Lisa L., Binder, Jeffrey R., and Rutvik, H. Desai. 2015. "Familiarity Differentially Affects Right Hemisphere Contributions to Processing Metaphors and Literals." *Frontiers in Human Neuroscience* 10: https://doi.org/10.3389/fnhum.2015.00044.

Laitman, Jeffrey T. 1983. "The Evolution of the Hominid Upper Respiratory System and Implications for the Origins of Speech." In E. de Grolier, ed., *Glossogenetics: The Origin and Evolution of Language*, pp. 63–90. Utrecht: Harwood.

Laitman, Jeffrey T. 1990. "Tracing the Origins of Human Speech." In P. Whitten and D. E. K. Hunter, eds., *Anthropology: Contemporary Perspectives*, pp. 124–130. Glenview, IL: Scott, Foresman and Company.

Lakoff, George. 1979. "The Contemporary Theory of Metaphor." In Andrew Ortony, ed., *Metaphor and Thought*, pp. 202–251. Cambridge: Cambridge University Press.

Lakoff, George. 1986. "The Meanings of Literal." *Metaphor and Symbolic Activity* 1: 291–296.

Lakoff, George .1987. *Women, Fire, and Dangerous Things: What Categories Reveal about the Mind.* Chicago: University of Chicago Press.

Lakoff, George, and Johnson, Mark. 1980: *Metaphors We Live By.* Chicago: University of Chicago Press.

Lakoff, George, and Johnson, Mark. 1999. *Philosophy in Flesh: The Embodied Mind and Its Challenge to Western Thought.* New York: Basic.

Lakoff, George, and Núñez, Rafael. 2000. *Where Mathematics Comes From: How the Embodied Mind Brings Mathematics into Being.* New York: Basic Books.

Lakoff, George, and Turner, Mark. 1989. *More than Cool Reason: A Field Guide to Poetic Metaphor.* Chicago: University of Chicago Press.

Langacker, Ronald W. 1987. *Foundations of Cognitive Grammar.* Stanford: Stanford University Press.

Langacker, Ronald W. 1990. *Concept, Image, and Symbol: The Cognitive Basis of Grammar.* Berlin: Mouton de Gruyter.

Langacker, Ronald W. 1999. *Grammar and Conceptualization.* Berlin: Mouton de Gruyter.

Langer, Susanne K. 1948. *Philosophy in a New Key.* New York: Mentor Books.

Lauand, Jean. 2009. "The Role of Riddles in Medieval Education." *Revista Internacional d'Humanitats* 16: 5–12.

Lapidge Michael, and Rosier, James L. 1985. *Aldhelm: The Poetic Works*. Cambridge: D. S. Brewer.
Lassner, Jacob. 1993. *Demonizing the Queen of Sheba: Boundaries of Gender and Culture in Postbiblical Judaism and Medieval Islam*. Chicago: University of Chicago Press.
Lear, Edward. 1846. *A Book of Nonsense*. London: Frederick Warne.
Lear, Edward. 1871. *Nonsense Songs, Stories, Botany, and Alphabets*. Boston: James R. Osgood.
Lear, Edward. 1877. *Laughable Lyrics*. London: R. J. Bush.
Leary, T. J. 2014. *Symphosius: The Aenigmata: An Introduction, Text and Commentary*. London: Bloomsbury.
Lent, Jeremy. 2017. *The Patterning Instinct: A Cultural History of Humanity's Search for Meaning*. New York: Prometheus.
Lévi-Strauss, Claude. 1962: *The Savage Mind*. London: Weidenfeld & Nicolson.
Lieberman, Philip. 1972. *The Speech of Primates*. The Hague: Mouton.
Lieberman, Philip. 1975. *On the Origins of Language*. New York: MacMillan.
Lieberman, Philip. 1984. *The Biology and Evolution of Language*. Cambridge, MA: Harvard University Press.
Lieberman, Philip. 1991. *Uniquely Human: The Evolution of Speech, Thought, and Selfless Behavior*. Cambridge, MA: Harvard University Press.
Lieberman, Philip. 2000. *Human Language and Our Reptilian Brain*. Cambridge, MA: Harvard University Press.
Locke, John. 1690. *An Essay Concerning Humane Understanding*, ed. P. H. Nidditch. Oxford: Clarendon Press.
Lotman, Yuri. 1991. *Universe of the Mind: A Semiotic Theory of Culture*. Bloomington: Indiana University Press.
Luo, Jing, and Niki, Kazuhisa. 2003. "Function of Hippocampus in Insight of Problem Solving." *Hippocampus* 13: 316–323.
Mâche, Francois-Bernard. 1993. *Music, Myth and Nature, or The Dolphins of Arion*. London: Routledge.
Magnus, Margaret. 1999. *Gods of the Word: Archetypes in the Consonants*. Kirksville, Missouri: Thomas Jefferson University Press.
Maier, Michael. 1617. *Atalanta Fugiens*. Oppenheim: Bry.
Malinowski, Bronislaw. 1922. *Argonauts of the Western Pacific*. New York: Dutton.
Malinowski, Bronislaw. 1923. "The Problem of Meaning in Primitive Languages." In Charles K. Ogden and I. A. Richards, eds., *The Meaning of Meaning*, pp. 296–336. New York: Harcourt, Brace and World.
McDowell, John H. 1979. *Children's Riddling*. Bloomington: Indiana University Press.
McGhee, Paul 2002. *Understanding and Promoting the Development of Children's Humor*. Dubuque: Kendall/Hunt.
McNeill, David. 1992. *Hand and Mind: What Gestures Reveal about Thought*. Chicago: University of Chicago Press
McNeill, David. 2005. *Gesture and Thought*. Chicago: University of Chicago Press.

Merleau-Ponty, Maurice. 1942. *La structure du comportement*. Paris: Presses Universitaires de France.
Merleau-Ponty, Maurice. 1945. *Phénomenologie de la perception*. Paris: Gallimard.
Metz, Christian. 1982. *The Imaginary Signifier*. Bloomington: Indiana University Press.
Migliorini, Bruno. 1987. *Storia della lingua italiana*. Firenze: Sansoni.
Milner, Richard. 1990. *The Encyclopedia of Evolution: Humanity's Search for Its Origins*. New York: Facts on File.
Mollica, Anthony. 2019 *Ludolinguistica: I giochi linguistici e la didattica dell'italiano*. Loreto: ELI Publishing.
Naerebout, Frederick G., and Beerden, Kim. 2013. "Gods Cannot Tell Lies: Riddling and Ancient Greek Divination." In J. Kwapzt, D. Petrain, and M. Szymanski, eds., *The Muse at Play: Riddles and Wordplay in Greek and Latin Poetry*, pp. 121–147. Berlin: Mouton de Gruyter.
Nietzsche, Friedrich. 1873. *Philosophy and Truth: Selections from Nietzsche's Notebooks of the Early 1870's*. Atlantic Heights, NJ: Humanities Press.
Nordal, Sigurdur, and Turville-Petre, G. 1960. *The Saga of King Heidrik the Wise*. London: Thomas Nelson and Sons.
Ong, Walter J. 1977. *Interfaces of the Word: Studies in the Evolution of Consciousness and Culture*. Ithaca: Cornell University Press.
Ortony, Andrew, ed. 1979. *Metaphor and Thought*. Cambridge: Cambridge University Press.
Paget, Richard. 1930. *Human Speech*. London: Kegan Paul.
Paton, William R. 1927. *The Greek Anthology*. London: William Heineman.
Peirce, Charles Sanders. 1931–1958: *Collected Writings*, 8 Vols. Cambridge: Harvard University Press.
Pepicello, William J., and Green, Thomas A. 1984. *The Language of Riddles: New Perspectives*. Columbus: Ohio State University Press.
Perrault, Charles. 1697. *Les contes de ma mere l'Oye*. Paris: Lamy.
Plato 1951. *The Symposium*. Harmondsworth: Penguin.
Plato 2013. *Cratylus*. Trans. by Benjamin Jowett. Project Gutenberg http:// https://www.gutenberg.org/ebooks/1616.
Pollio, Howard R., Barlow, Jack M., Fine, Harold J., and Pollio, Marilyn R. 1977. *The Poetics of Growth: Figurative Language in Psychology, Psychotherapy, and Education*. Hillsdale, NJ: Lawrence Erlbaum.
Pollio, Howard and Burns, Barbara. 1977. "The Anomaly of Anomaly." *Journal of Psycholinguistic Research* 6: 247–260.
Pollio, Howard and Smith, Michael. 1979. "Sense and Nonsense in Thinking About Anomaly and Metaphor." *Bulletin of the Psychonomic Society* 13: 323–326.
Popper, Karl. 1976. *The Unending Quest*. Glasgow: Collins.
Popper, Karl, and Eccles, John. 1977. *The Self and the Brain*. Berlin: Springer.
Postle, Bradley R. 2016. "The Hippocampus, Memory, and Consciousness." In S. Laureys, O. Grosseries, and G. Tononi, eds., *The Neurology of Consciousness*, pp. 349–363. New York: Academic.

Potamiti, Anna. 2015. "Playing at Riddles in Greek." *Greek, Roman, and Byzantine Studies* 55: 133–153.

Purser, H., Van Herwegen, J., and Thomas, M. 2020. "The Development of Children's Comprehension and Appreciation of Riddles." *Journal of Experimental Child Psychology* 189: 104709.

Quintilian. 1875. *Institutio Oratoria*. Trans. J. S. Watson. London: George Bell and Sons.

Reddy, Michael J. 1979. "The Conduit Metaphor: A Case of Frame Conflict in Our Language about Language." In A. Ortony, ed., *Metaphor and Thought*, pp. 284–310. Cambridge: Cambridge University Press.

Richards, I. A. 1936. *The Philosophy of Rhetoric*. Oxford: Oxford University Press.

Rickman, H. P. 2004. *The Riddle of the Sphinx: Interpreting the Human World*. Cranbury: Associated University Presses.

Ross, Phillip E. 1991. "Hard Words." *Scientific American* 264/4: 138–147.

Rousseau, Jean Jacques. 1966. *Essay on the Origin of Language*. Chicago: University of Chicago Press.

Rudolph, Richard C. 1942. "Notes on the Riddle in China." *California Folklore Quarterly* 1: 65–82.

Salomon, Richard. 1996. "When Is a Riddle Not a Riddle? Some Comments on Riddling and Related Poetic Devices in Classical Sanskrit." In G. Hasan-Rokem and D. Shulman, eds., *Untying the Knot: On Riddles and Other Enigmatic Modes*, pp. 168–178. Oxford: Oxford University Press.

Sapir, Edward. 1921. *Language*. New York: Harcourt, Brace, and World.

Saussure, Ferdinand de. 1916 *Cours de linguistique générale*. Paris: Payot.

Schiltz, Katelijne. 2015. *Music and Riddle Culture in the Renaissance*. Cambridge: Cambridge University Press.

Schmidt, Gwenda L., and Seger, Carol A. 2009. "Neural Correlates of Metaphor Processing: The Roles of Figurativeness, Familiarity and Difficulty." *Brain and Cognition* 71: 375–386.

Schuessler, Axel. 2007 *ABC Etymological Dictionary of Old Chinese*. Honolulu: University of Hawaii Press.

Scott, Charles T. 1965. *Persian and Arabic Riddles: A Language-Centered Approach to Genre Definition*. The Hague: Mouton.

Sebeok, Thomas A., and Danesi, Marcel. 2000. *The Forms of Meaning: Modeling Systems Theory and Semiotics*. Berlin: Mouton de Gruyter.

Sebo, Erin. 2009. "Was Symphosius an African? A Contextualizing Note on Two Textual Clues in the *Aenigmata Symphosii*." *Notes & Queries* 56: 324–326.

Sebo, Erin. 2018. *In Enigmate: The History of a Riddle, 400–1500*. Dublin: Four Courts Press.

Senderovich, Savely. 2005. *The Riddle of the Riddle*. London: Routledge.

Seyeb-Gohrab, A. A. 2010. *Courtly Riddles: Enigmatic Embellishments in Early Persian Poetry*. Leiden: Leiden University Press.

Shah, Amina. 1980. *The Assemblies of Al-Hariri: Fifty Encounters with the Shaykh Abu Zayd of Serju*. London: Octagon.

Shevoroshkin, Vitaly. 1990. "The Mother Tongue." *The Sciences* 30: 20–27.

Silverman, Kaja. 1983: *The Subject of Semiotics*. New York: Oxford University Press.
Sorrell, Paul. 1996. "Alcuin's Comb Riddle." *Neophilologicus* 80: 311–318.
*Spelling Books*. Internet Archive, https://archive.org/stream/spellingforgrades_202002/simplificationof00harl_djvu.txt.
Stam, James. 1976. *Inquiries in the Origin of Language: The Fate of a Question*. New York: Harper and Row.
Sternberg, Robert J. 1985. *Beyond IQ: A Triarchic Theory of Human Intelligence*. New York: Cambridge University Press.
Stross, Brian. 1976. *The Origin and Evolution of Language*. Dubuque, Iowa: W.C. Brown.
Sullivan, Karen S. 2007. *Grammar in Metaphor: A Construction Grammar Account of Metaphoric Language*, Doctoral thesis, University of Berkeley.
Swadesh, Morris. 1951. "Diffusional Cumulation and Archaic Residue as Historical Explanations." *Southwestern Journal of Anthropology* 7: 1–21.
Swadesh, Morris. 1959. "Linguistics as an Instrument of Prehistory." *Southwestern Journal of Anthropology* 15: 20–35.
Swadesh, Morris. 1971. *The Origins and Diversification of Language*. Chicago: Aldine-Atherton.
Swaminatham, Santanam. 2014. "Oldest Riddle in the World." *Sparkingtree.in*: https://www.speakingtree.in/blog/oldest-riddle-in-the-world-rig-veda-mystery-3.
Sweetser, Eve. 1990. *From Etymology to Pragmatics: Metaphorical and Cultural Aspects of Semantic Structure*. Cambridge: Cambridge University Press.
Symphosius. *The Hundred Riddles of Symphosius*. Internet Archive, https://archive.org/stream/hundredriddless00sympgoog/hundredriddless00sympgoog_djvu.txt.
Taplin, Oliver. 1985. *Greek Tragedy in Action*. London: Routledge.
Taylor, Archer. 1948. *The Literary Riddle Before 1600*. Berkeley: University of California Press.
Taylor, Archer. 1951. *English Riddles from Oral Tradition*. Berkeley: University of California Press.
Tenniel, John. 2003. *Alice's Adventures in Wonderland and Through the Looking-Glass*. London: Penguin Classics.
Tolkein, J. R. (1937). *The Hobbit*. Internet Archive, https://archive.org/details/dli.ernet.474126.
Tsur, Reuven .1992. *What Makes Sound Patterns Expressive? The Poetic Mode of Speech Perception*. Durham: Duke University Press.
Tupper, Frederick. 1903. "Originals and Analogues of the Exeter Book Riddles." *Modern Language Notes* 18: 97–106.
Turner, Mark. 1997. *The Literary Mind*. Oxford: Oxford University Press.
Turner, Mark, and Fauconnier, Gilles. 1995. "Conceptual Integration and Formal Expression." *Metaphor and Symbolic Activity* 10: 183–204.
Tylor, Edward B. 1871. *Primitive Culture*. London: Murray.
Uexküll, Jakob von. 1909. *Umwelt und Innenwelt der Tierre*. Berlin: Springer.
Uther, Hans-Jörg. 2006. "The Fox in World Literature: Reflections on a Fictional Animal." *Asian Folklore Studies* 65: 133–160.

Vatuk, Prakash. 1969. "Amir Khusro and Indian Riddle Tradition." *The Journal of American Folklore* 82: 142–154.
Verene, Donald P. 1981. *Vico's Science of Imagination*. Ithaca: Cornell University Press.
Vinci, Leonardo da.1519 *Codex Atlanticus*. Milan: Biblioteca Ambrosiana.
Voltaire. *The Project Gutenberg eBook of Voltaire's Romances*, Project Gutenberg, https://www.gutenberg.org/files/35595/35595.txt.
Vygotsky, Lev S. 1962. *Thought and Language*. Cambridge, MA: MIT Press.
Vygotsky, Lev S. 1978. *Mind in Society*. Cambridge: Cambridge University Press.
Wells, David. 1988. *Hidden Connections, Double Meanings: A Mathematical Exploration*. Cambridge: Cambridge University Press.
Wells, David. 1995. *You Are a Mathematician*. Harmondsworth: Penguin.
Wescott, Roger. 1980. *Sound and Sense*. Lake Bluff: Jupiter Press.
White, Hayden. 1973. *Metahistory: The Historical Imagination in Nineteenth-Century Europe*. Baltimore: Johns Hopkins University Press.
White, Hayden. 1978: *Tropics of Discourse: Essays in Cultural Criticism*. Baltimore: Johns Hopkins University Press.
Whorf, Benjamin Lee. 1941. "The Relation of Habitual Thought to Language." In Leslie Spier, ed., *Language, Culture, and Personality: Essays in Memory of Edward Sapir*, pp. 75–93. Menasha: Sapir Memorial Publication Fund.
Whorf, Benjamin Lee. 1956. *Language, Thought, and Reality*, John B. Carroll ed. Cambridge: MIT Press.
Williams, Sidney, Madan, Falconer, and Green, Roger. 1962. *Lewis Carroll Handbook*. Oxford: Oxford University Press.
Winner, Ellen 1982. *Invented Worlds: The Psychology of the Arts*. Cambridge, MA: Harvard University Press.
Wittgenstein, Ludwig. 1922. *Tractatus Logico-Philosophicus*. London: Routledge and Kegan Paul.
Wittgenstein, Ludwig. 1953. *Philosophical Investigations*. New York: Macmillan.
Wittgenstein, Ludwig. 1969. *On Certainty*. London: Blackwell.
Worde, Wynkyn de 1511. *Demaundes Joyous*. Reprint 1829. Thomas White publisher.
Wundt, Wilhelm. 1901. *Sprachgeschichte und Sprachpsychologie*. Leipzig: Eugelmann.
Wynkyn de Worde. 1511. *Demaundes Joyous*. Held in the Cambridge University Library.
Yalisove, Daniel. 1978. "The Effect of Riddle Structure on Children's Comprehension of Riddles." *Developmental Psychology* 14: 173–180.
Zhang, Dongyu, Zhang, Minghao, Peng, Ciyuan, and Jung, Jason. 2021. "Metaphor Research in the 21st Century: A Bibliographic Analysis." *Computer Science and Information Systems* 18: 1–21.

# Index

Page references for figures and tables are italicized.

abduction, 63, 64, 66, 69
abstraction, 2, 6, 15, 17, 19, 22, 29, 37, 63, 67, 75, 83, 87, 88, 108, 114
*Aenigmata Symphosii*, 9, 42, 43
African riddles, 91–92
age of the gods, heroes, and equals, 65
Alcuin, 11, 45–46
Aldhelm, 10, *13*, 46–47
Al-Hariri of Basra, 11, *13*
*Alice's Adventures in Wonderland*, 54
analogy, 26, 101, 104, 105
Aquinas, Thomas, 20
Aristotle, 15, 18, 19, 68
Arnheim, Rudolf, 66, 80
Asch, Solomon, 23
Austen, Jane, 52
Aztec riddles, 92

Babylonian mythology, 124
Babylonian riddles, 27, 58, 88, 98, 101, 106, 119
Bertoldo, 57
bicamerality, 71, 84, 107, 121–24
bimodality, 71
Black, Max, 23, 25
blending, 23, 26, 55, 74, 77, 81, 84, 89, 96, 99–100

Bühler, Karl, 22

Canning, George, 52
Carroll, Lewis, 11–12, 14, 50–51, 54–55
Cassirer, Ernst, 6
Castiglione, Baldassare, 49
Chagga, 22
charade, 11, 13, 42, 50, 52, 57
childhood, 5, 34, 43, 64, 73, 84, 94, 114
Chinese mythology, 9; riddles, 93
Chomsky, Noam, 26–27
Cicero, 19–20, 82
clustering, 28, 88, 90, 106, 116
cognition, 2, 6, 20, 70–74, 80, 81, 83, 94, 100, 105, 120, 121–23, 126
conceptual metaphor, 19, 24, 75, 76, 79, 81, 87, 94, 96, 117; conceptual metaphor theory, 3, 18, 25, 26–29, 63, 68–70, 72, 78, 84–87, 94, 97, 101, 102, 105, 106, 107, 125
conceptualization, 8, 9, 18, 24, 29, 31, 79, 107, 111, 123, 127
consciousness, 33, 61, 65, 70–74, 83, 84, 117–24
conundrum, 11, 12, 13, 48, 50, 53, 57
*corso*, 65
culture, 5, 8, 14–15, 22, 33, 65, 107

Danforth, Samuel, 12
Dante, 70
De Bono, Edward, 58
delectation, 3, 36, 41, 42, 45, 48, 81, 87
*Demaundes Joyous*, 48
destiny, 2, 38, 67, 102, 122
discourse, 3, 6, 9, 11–14, 20, 21, 30, 31, 35–37, 41, 42, 46, 50, 56, 68, 70, 93, 94, 106, 108, 110
*Divine Comedy*, 70

echoism, 31–32, 111–12
Eco, Umberto, 18
Egyptian mythology, 124, 128
enigma, 11–13, 35, 42, 43, 50, 52, 57
event structure, 70–71, 78, 86, 99, 102–5, 119
*Exeter Book*, 10, *13*, 47

fable, 21, 36, 68, 85, 123, 124
fairy tale, 13, 42, 53
*fantasia*, 62–63, 66–69, 77, 81, 120, 121
Fauconnier, Gilles, 7, 26, 74
folk wisdom, 35, 36
frame, 94–95, 97
Frye, Northrop, 30, 72

Gestalt psychology, 22–23
gesticulant, 116–17
gesture, 31–33, 107, 112–13, 116–17
Gollum's riddles, 16–17
grammar, 6, 77–80, 85, 97, 112, 124, 126
*Greek Anthology*, 39–40, 42
Greek mythology, 15, 124
Greek riddle, 88
ground (metaphorical), 23–24

Hindu literature, 15, 43
Hobbes, Thomas, 20–21
Hovanec, Helene, 36, 42
Huizinga, Johan, 35
humor, 14, 35, 42, 48, 49, 56

iconicity, 31–32, 78, 84, 111, 114, 116, 117, 120–21, 124, 126
image schema, 28, 40–41, 57, 67, 77, 80, 83, 87, 89, 91–96, 98, 100, 105, 117, 123, 124, 126
*Indovinello veronese*, 44–45
*ingegno*, 62, 63, 81, 120
interactionist model, 23–24
invariance, 71, 96, 102, 105
irony, 15, 30, 68, 93–94, 125

Jabberwocky, 55–56
Jaynes, Julian, 5, 15, 71, 84, 107, 121–23
Jespersen, Otto, 31, 115
Johnson, Mark, 18, 26, 28, 70–71, 76, 87, 123

Kant, Immanuel, 21, 126
Köngas-Maranda, Elli, 13, 38, 88, 91

Laitman, Jeffrey, 113
Lakoff, George, 7, 8, 18, 21, 24, 26, 28, 70–71, 76, 85, 87, 96, 102–5, 108, 125, 127
Langacker, Ronald, 80
Langer, Susanne, 77
language versus speech, 1, 5, 6, 31–33, 61, 78–81, 84, 105, 107–15, 122, 124
larynx, 113
lateral thinking, 58
layering, 81, 83, 87, 94–101, 104, 106, 107, 123, 126
Lear, Edward, 56
Lieberman, Philip, 113
limerick, 56
literal language, 16, 18–27, 37, 58, 68–69, 79, 80, 108, 124
literary function, 3, 7, 9, 10, 11, 13, 35, 36, 42, 47, 48–50, 81, 107
literary nonsense, 53–54, 56
Locke, John, 20, 71, 115
*lógos*, 15, 42, 62
ludic function, 3, 7, 8, 10, 13, 14, 30, 35, 36, 41, 42, 56, 59, 107, 120

Mad Hatter's riddle, 54
Magnus, Margaret, 116
Malinowski, Bronislaw, 15, 110
mapping, 6, 8, 18, 19, 26, 29, 30, 39, 41, 59, 63, 64, 66, 68–71, 74, –78, 83–91, 94, 96, 101, 102, 104, 105, 109, 114, 123, 127
McDowell, John, 58
McNeill, David, 116–17
*memoria*, 62–63, 65, 72, 81, 82, 121
*The Merry Book of Riddles*, 48–49
metaphor, 2–3, 5–6, 9, 17, 18, 21, 64; clustering 27–28; interactionist model, 23–24; journey metaphors, 15, 28, 29, 59, 70, 83, 89, 100; phase metaphors, 6–8, 16–17, 26, 65, 70, 78, 83, 85–86, 96; primary metaphor, 8, 9; root metaphor, 8, 14–15, 17, 37, 65, 120; time metaphors, 8, 26, 27, 79; vision metaphors, 27, 29, 87, 88, 90; year metaphors, 16, 27, 85, 88. *See also* conceptual metaphor
metaphor hypothesis, 2–3, 6, 7, 15–16, 31, 34, 73–81, 84, 124–28
metaphysical function, 3, 6–9, 13, 15, 17, 30, 33, 36, 59, 89
metonymy, 30, 68, 84, 93, 94, 124, 125
myth, 2–7, 13, 18, 33, 65, 82, 98, 102, 110, 124; Pandora myth, 105
*mythos*, 15, 42, 62, 109

naming, 1, 5, 6, 17, 64, 68, 84, 110, 112
narrative, 6, 14, 33, 38, 63, 65, 84, 85, 124
*New Science*, 61, 124
Nietzsche, Friedrich, 21
nomination, 31, 34, 36, 61, 84, 105, 107–11, 112, 114, 120
nonsense (anomalous) string, 26–27
Norse mythology, 15, 40, 90; Norse riddles, 40–41, 90, 101
Nostratic, 31, 32
nursery rhyme, 13, 42, 53

Oedipus myth, 2, 6–8, 30, 36–38, 83, 100, 102–4, 126–27, 128
ontogeny, 5, 34, 64, 65, 113, 114
ontological function, 6, 19, 68, 85, 106, 122
oracles, 5, 7, 30, 38, 59; Oracle at Delphi, 6, 30, 36, 37, 83
origin of language, 2, 15, 121; origin of speech, 2, 111, 115

Paget, Richard, 33, 112
pedagogical function, 3, 7, 9–11, 13, 30, 35, 36, 42, 56–59, 81, 87, 120
Peirce, Charles S., 63, 114, 120, *121*, 126
Perrault, Charles, 53
personification, 9, 43, 68, 98–101, 104
Philippine mythology, 38; Philippine riddles, 93
philology, 1, 6
phylogeny, 5, 34, 64, 113, 114
Plato, 42–43, 69, 70, 88, 115
poetic logic, 21, 61–67, 69–75, 77, 81, 82, 83, 96, 105, 110, 122, 124, 126
poetic wisdom, 62–66, 69–71, 73, 77, 81, 82, 105, 124
Pollio, Howard, 26, 27
Popper, Karl, 120, *121*
Proto-Indo-European (PIE), 31, 32
proverbs, 22, 29, 30, 39, 104, 105

Queen of Sheba, 39
Quintilian, 19

radiation, 106
reconstruction, 111, 114
recreation function, 6, 9, 10, 13, 41, 48
Reddy, Michael, 94–95, 117
Richards, I. A., 23
*ricorso*, 65
riddle, 2, 5, 6–15, 35, 64, 94, 100, 126–28; literary, 3, 6, 7, 9, 10, 11, 13, 30, 35, 36, 42, 47, 48–50, 52, 53, 54, 56, 70, 72, 75, 81, 107; ludic, 5, 7, 9, 10, 13, 14, 30, 35, 36, 41,

42, 56, 59, 107, 120; metaphysical, 3, 6–9, 13, 14, 15, 17, 30, 33, 36, 40, 53, 59, 73, 87, 89, 93; mythic, 13–14, 15, 16, 17, 35–38, 42, 59, 66, 88, 109; pedagogical, 3, 7, 9–10, 13, 30, 35, 36, 42, 56–59, 107, 120; phenomenological, 17, 29, 40, 41, 57, 75, 84, 89, 107, 111; riddle joke, 35; situation-specific, 9, 10, 29, 36, 40, 46, 49, 75, 86, 87, 100
Riddle of the Sphinx, 2, 6–9, *13*, 16, 18, 24, 26, 36, 37, 39, 64, 66, 70, *72*, 78, 83, 85, 87, 96, 100, 102, 105–6, 119, 124, 126–28
Rousseau, Jean-Jacques, 32, 33, 113, 117

Samson's riddle, 38–39
Sanskrit riddles, 16, 27, 37, 39, 85, 91
Saturnalia, 10, 13, 41, 42
Saussure, Ferdinand de, 110–11, 115
Sebo, Erin, 10, 36
sense implication, 68, 74, 76–79, 81, 84
Socrates, 15, 115
Sophocles, 7, 36, 127
sound symbolism, 31, 114–16
source domain, 26, 30, 37, 39, 41, 45, 49, 64, 67, 69, 70, 71, 76–80, 84, 86, 87–96, 100, 106, 128
Swadesh, Morris, 32, 112, 115

Sweetser, Eve, 2–3, 29
Symphosius, 9, 10, *13*, 42, 43, 47
symposium, 6, 42, 43

*Tales of My Mother Goose*, 42, 53–54
target domain, 26, 30, 64, 69, 71, 76, 78, 84, 87, 88, 90, 94, 96
Taylor, Archer, 40, 58
tenor (topic), 23
*Through the Looking-Glass*, 54
Turner, Mark, 7, 26, 74, 105
Tylor, Edward B., 107

understanding function, 36–41

vehicle, 23–25
Verene, Donald, 62
Vico, Giambattista, 13, 15–16, 21, 25, 26, 61–63, 65–66, 68–69, 73, 74, 78, 81, 107, 117
Vinci, Leonardo da, 49
Voltaire, 49–50
Vygotsky, Lev S., 34, 64, 124

Walpole, Horace, 52
Whorf, Benjamin Lee, 71, 115–16, 120–21
Wittgenstein, Ludwig, 12, 37, 59–60
Wundt, Wilhelm, 22

# About the Author

**Marcel Danesi** is professor emeritus of linguistic anthropology at the University of Toronto. He was director of the program in semiotics at the same university. He has published extensively in linguistics and semiotics, including the following recent books: *The Semiotics of Emojis* (2016), *Linguistic Relativity Today* (2021), and *Warning Signs: The Semiotics of Danger* (2022).

www.ingramcontent.com/pod-product-compliance
Lightning Source LLC
Chambersburg PA
CBHW020125010526
44115CB00008B/982